Dying For the Light

By

Barbara Jean Lindsey

Cosmic Barbara Books are available for order through
Ingram Press Catalogues

Barbara Jean Lindsey
Visit my website at www.BarbaraJeanLindsey.com

Printed in the United States of America
First Printing: May 2016
Published by Sojourn Publishing, LLC

ISBN: 978-1-62747-206-7
Ebook ISBN: 978-1-62747-207-4

Dedicated to my beloved children,
Ryan, Melody and Audrey

Introduction

In 1989 I had a near death experience, "NDE," that changed my life forever. From that point, I continued on a spiritual quest for over twenty-five years to find out who I was and why I was here. While traveling to many of the world's sacred sites, I was very fortunate to meet many amazing teachers, healers, and masters, and be given knowledge and initiations in ancient traditions. Upon those traditions,

Dying for the Light was imagined into existence.

People are curious about what happens when we die. Is there life after death? Will I be reunited with my loved ones?

This is my true story of a near death experience that took me on a journey to the Afterlife and back again. After the near death experience (NDE), my original life was irrevocably changed forever.

I knocked on Death's door, and when she opened it, I re-discovered that I continued to exist even without a body. I learned I come from love, I am love, I will return to love, and I never die.

I had been raised to fear death. I have replaced those illusions of fear, and learned to trust the mysteries of this process.

I crossed that doorway to the afterlife and discovered that death is not such a great big mystery after all, but instead a part of an intelligent spiral of birth, life, death, and rebirth, created and lovingly aligned organically with my best interest at heart.

I was given a gift of the final journey from this world to the next, and I learned that it is a glorious, ancient rite of passage that all human beings will experience.

This knowledge is the gift I brought back for you.

"When death is regarded not (as with us) as an ultimate dissolution, but rather as a transitional (and crucial) stage of a journey, then the apparent Egyptian preoccupation with death becomes exactly the opposite of what it seems to be. It is, in fact, a preoccupation with life in the deepest possible sense."

John Anthony West
<u>Serpent in the Sky</u>

Foreword

I was introduced to Barbara Jean, by a good friend, at a conference in San Francisco. Just before she was about to serve on a UFO/ET panel, at that conference, Barbara Jean briefly shared with me her extraordinary near death experience. Years later, I met up with her again at a Twilight Brigade weekend training that she'd decided to attend. As a hospice volunteer for 40 years, and the co-founder of The Twilight Brigade (my non-profit organization that trains volunteers to be at the bedside of those in transition), I was sincerely touched by Barbara Jean's huge heart. I sensed she was reclaiming her personal power through her service to humanity. I believe writing this book is also a part of her life mission.

Barbara Jean's book, Dying for the Light, offers unique yet, deeply genuine insights of her near death, out of this world journey! She conveys her experience in such great detail you will feel yourself magically transported right into the event with her. As a single mother of three, Barbara Jean writes with the practical down-to-earth, humorous perspective only the challenges of daily family life could have taught her.

In Dying for the Light, Barbara Jean describes what it was like for her to die, and to be taken to the Other Side, where she became a student of the Cosmos. Like all mighty storytellers, she weaves the lessons of love and transformation throughout the sharing of her near death experience, in order to create a beautiful story carefully threaded on a tapestry of hope and inspiration.

I have had many conversations with the late Dr. John Mack, a psychiatrist, and professor at Harvard. He was a leading authority of the spiritual transformational affects of alien abductions and near death experiences. He shared with me similar stories that he uncovered in his regression therapy. By supporting this book, my hopes are that it may encourage others to come forward with their stories and to bring a greater awareness of this phenomenon.

Without a doubt, Barbara Jean's encounters in the Afterlife, and the wisdom she returned with, will truly transform your life and expand your consciousness.

Dannion Brinkley
NY Times Best Selling Author
Near Death Experiencer

Contents

One of the Lucky Ones

"I want nachos and I want them now!" I declared at the top of my lungs, as I bolted upright in my hospital bed, fully awake and completely aware of the tremendous journey I had just experienced. Not the most profound first raspy words, when coming out of a coma, but I was starving. Dying apparently leaves you hungry.

It was December 4, 1989 and I had been lying silently in a comatose state in a small hospital bed in a state of deep and prolonged unconsciousness – not moving, not speaking coherently, for two days – when suddenly I awakened. My body sprang into a straight and upright sitting position, like a rubber band stretched too tight right before it snaps. My shouting out loud had shattered the cold silence of the private hospital room. My sudden movements automatically tugged on all the attached monitor cords. The room was suddenly filled with a merry-go-round of apocalyptic flashing red lights and sirens.

Cindy, my best friend at the time, reacted with complete shock, as she was jerked out of her bedside vigil of silent meditation and prayer. She stared up at me with her dark brown eyes, like a deer caught in the headlights, and cried out as she leaped from her chair, "Oh, my God! You are back. You are alive. How are you? Are you okay? Oh, my God!" She jumped up and down with exuberant excitement. "You can even talk!" Up until that very moment, the expectation of my death had been imminent.

Two days earlier, I had been rushed to the hospital emergency room in an ambulance, unable to breathe, in severe distress, and rapidly deteriorating. Both my lungs had collapsed, and I was slipping into a comatose state. I had been intubated and paralyzed as extreme emergency measures to save my life.

My family and friends had been told that I was continuing to fight for my life, but the odds of my making it were dismal to say the least, and getting more and more life-threatening by the minute. Could I hang on? Would I make it? The doctors didn't want to give anyone false hope.

Being in a coma-like condition and lying in the hospital bed hooked up to all those machines, I must have looked like a sack of potatoes just lying there. Not being able to talk, walk, or do anything physical for myself, I appeared to be mostly dead. My body was there, but I had checked out. I had no personality present, and I kind of have a big personality if you get to know me. Machines were breathing, eating, and drinking for me. I had no knowledge of what had happened to me, or so it seemed to my family and friends, because I couldn't talk to them even if I had wanted to.

My family and the doctors agreed that everything possible had been done, and all anyone could do now was to wait, pray, and hope for the best. It was surely out of the doctors' hands.

Cindy explained to me that my husband, immediate family, and close friends were waiting in the corridor just outside my room. They had all rushed to the emergency room upon hearing the frightening news, and together they had kept a round-the-clock vigil for my safekeeping.

"Where are my children? Who is taking care of them? Are they okay?" Being a fierce mother who protects her young, I needed to know how my children were doing before I could relax about anything else. Cindy assured me that my children were in good hands with family and friends, now and during the time I had been comatose.

I was awake and acting as though I had just gotten up from a short nap, instead of knocking down death's door and passing back through again. Not only was I talking as though nothing had ever happened, but I was also sitting straight up in my hospital bed, demanding something to eat. I talked excitedly with Cindy, asking how everyone was doing and trying my best to be filled in on what I had missed. It was a combination of divine intervention, Western medicine, and man's machines that had kept me alive.

During my first few days after waking up in the hospital, various doctors, nurses, and specialists examined me, checked my charts and tests, and continuously asked me questions about how I was feeling. I was prodded and poked for samples of blood and urine, x-rayed, and fed drugs for asthma and pain. The doctors, overall, were generally very kind, and genuinely intrigued with me.

The hospital routines continued, and after the first few days, to the amazement of everyone, I seemed to be out of harm's way and, surprisingly, healing rather quickly. Having had such a close call with death, my progress was truly a miracle.

My cup was flowing over with love for life and for everyone in general, including my love for my family, for my friends and even for people I met for the first time. I was out of control with love. I wanted to hug people. I mean the deep, meaningful kind of hug, where you really connect with people spirit-to-spirit and eye-to-eye, with no more hiding of one's heart. Love was a side effect of my near death experience (NDE).

I felt more alive now than I ever had before the NDE. I was back – and I was excited about life. All of the previous worries, stresses, and financial pressures just didn't seem to be that important anymore. I had re-discovered such thankfulness and gratefulness for the gift of life – and the opportunities to experience such love would put me into exalted states of bliss. Glowing from the inside with all of that newly found love from having almost died, I had become a charged force of love to be reckoned with.

I thought to myself that the most satisfying thing about the whole journey up until that very moment was the realization that I am so much love, and that I have so much love to share – and that this made me so very happy to be alive. I decided that I would take that pow-er of the love that is in me and all around me, on this planet and throughout the Cosmos, and help change the things that need changing, and restore and rejuvenate the world as I knew it.

I would not be doing this work alone. This is be-cause I had learned that the power of love must be given away, without ego and self-interest, to really be set free to do its thing, and do what it is divinely, and uniquely, inspired to do. That is when the fun began after my NDE.

With that first hug of acknowledgement, I felt divinely connected to each and every person that I met – whether it was a nurse, technician or old friend who had come to visit me in my hospital room. I also realized that we were all connected to our beautiful planet, and to the Cosmos herself. That was a new and expanded thinking process that I had brought back from the other side.

I was beginning to realize that I had an "out of this world" story to tell. Would anyone believe me? Was it a dream, or worse yet, just my imagination or even a hallucination? Had I gone completely off the deep end? These questions quickly began to haunt my thinking. I kept silent about it, and that wasn't my nature. Astrologically speaking, and according to my birth chart, I have a Leo Sun, Leo Moon and a Pisces Rising sign. We generally love to talk, express ourselves, and be the center of attention most of the time.

I didn't confide in the doctors, nurses, or staff anything about my NDE story. I didn't feel confident in how they would respond to me, as I had not figured it all out yet, and I was still struggling myself to wrap my brain around it all. I attempted to tell one of the young doctors my story, but before I could really get into it, he very quickly suggested that I should talk to my minister or priest.

My hospital records concluded that death was imminent that night, and that my recovery was truly extraordinary. All signs were "go," so far. Many of the doctors told me repeatedly that I was "one of the lucky ones" to have come so close to death and then be able to make it back again – and that this was truly a miracle. They agreed that as far as they could tell, after extensive examinations and testing, that I would be free from any long-term side effects of my near death experience – at least physically. In just about all other ways, however, as I would discover later, I was irrevocably changed forever.

Everything Is Going To Be Okay

The head nurse attending me was very efficient and friendly. Vigorously fluffing up my pillow and checking my vital signs, she whispered softly into my right ear, "You gave everyone quite a scare." I think it had been about three days, and I asked the nurse if I could take a bath. I had an overwhelming desire to be in warm water. I must have been feeling better, because I just wanted to wash my hair and smell sweet again. She returned much later that day, or was it night? The days and nights seemed rather mixed up to me, due to my dozing in and out.

We made our way down the bright hallway outside my room. Steadily we traveled like a ship in a storm down the corridor, balancing ever so lightly against the wall for support. I was surprised to find myself physically in a very weakened state, and I could barely walk, even with all the assistance. Yet my spirit had become so valiantly strong.

I had been an interior decorator before the NDE, so I had developed an eye for color and composition. In the middle of the austere room that we entered sat a grand, white, oversized Victorian-style claw foot bathtub. I stayed in the warm bathwater for hours and hours. I began to meditate in what I called my "incubator from heaven." My body had been put through so many electric shocks while the doctors were trying to save me that I was literally fried on the inside, and there wasn't one part of me that didn't ache or feel sore. I felt like I did when I had a sore throat, only it was my entire body that was sore. As I began to let the warm water heal my physical body, I began to feel safely nurtured once again.

The highlight of my ongoing recovery was when my dear friend, Debbie, smuggled my three children, along with her two small children and her six-month-old baby, into the hospital to visit me. I had called her and begged her to bring my children to me. I missed them terribly. How she got past the security station with all those children during non-visiting hours, and around the intensive-care staff of nurses, was beyond me. I was so happy to see my children's beautiful faces light up the moment they saw me. I loved them so much, and I was so thankful to still be a part of their lives. We all hugged and wept with joy. They brought my favorite flowers – daisies and roses – and their concerned faces. We all agreed that I would come home as soon as possible – and that yesterday would not be soon enough.

We were making a lot of noise, hugging and talking, and the girls climbed up onto the bed to cuddle in close beside me. My son laid his lanky arms and legs along the bottom of the bed and propped one of my pillows under his head. We talked for hours. As usual, it wasn't long before we started laughing and joking.

Then the night nurse peeked her head in the door, gave a stern look our way, and asked everyone to leave immediately. We all started instantaneously laughing out loud in unison. "The party's over," Debbie sang, as she began to put coats on all the children, picked up her baby and purse, and hugged me goodbye.

They all finally left when the timing was right. I could hear them all quietly laughing, whispering, and trying very hard to be inconspicuous – like a herd of bulls in a china shop – all the way down the outside corridor past my room, until I heard the sound of the elevator bell being pushed. I was thankful that everything was going to be okay, just as the head nurse had assured me.

Talking in Tongues

I had a heightened sense of taste, and the traditional hospital food that I was being served was not even anywhere close to being satisfying. I had been recovering in the hospital for about a week, when I convincingly begged and pleaded with my dear friend, Priscilla, to sneak in an order of nachos into the hospital for me.

She came bounding into my room with an unusually large purse, and proceeded to pull out, as if by magic, a big batch of piping hot nachos. We both laughed hysterically. We ate and talked, and I reassured her that despite all the rumors and gossip, I was going to be just fine, with no lasting negative side effects from the NDE. Old friends are the best. They are always there when you need them, no matter what the circumstances.

It was against hospital rules for me to eat anything that was not on my "safe" diet. Nachos were not on that "safe" list. I swear they were the best-tasting nachos I had ever eaten in my entire life. I devoured them the way a hungry bear would. How the small things in life can be so satisfying. I was truly looking at life very much through a child's eyes, open in wonder and discovery of everything – including all of my senses.

Feeling rather sleepy after pigging out on nachos, and still trying to make sense of what had happened to me, I reflected back to my childhood remembering my diverse religious upbringing. I would go to the Baptist church on my mom's side of the family and study the

Jehovah's Witness Book on my dad's side. Talk about a mixed bag.

On Friday nights, an event not to be missed was *"Talking in Tongues."* My two sisters and I used to sit in the front pew of the whitewashed Baptist church, so that we could get a good view of our neighbors as they would line up to be touched by the Holy Spirit. The same ordinary quiet neighbors we would say hello to as they went about their daily routines would be hit in the head and heart by the power of the Holy Spirit and transformed into outrageous jumping, yelling, and screaming fools. They would dance out of control, shaking, and convulsing, finally falling to the floor into a sleep like trance until it came to an end. Then they would simply get up, and walk to their seats in the pew, as though nothing had ever happened.

My sisters and I used to fake it that we were filled with the Holy Spirit when we weren't, so that the preacher would leave us alone. It was our amusement for the evening, since we were there against our teenage wills.

The preacher would stand up on the stage with a huge black Bible in his left hand, and he would get all worked up shouting and singing, all the while praising Jesus. He would preach about sinning, healing, casting out demons, and the temptations of the devil. He would begin to feel the Holy Spirit come through him; you could see his body shake and his brow sweat. Invariably, he would take his clean, white, starched handkerchief and sop up his wet skin, then put it back into the pocket of his pants and continue to preach the Word.

With a wild look in his eyes, he would begin to jump around in a very animated way, accentuating his words with volume, and passion.

The piano playing, the electric guitars strumming, and the drum beating, together with a whole church load of people joyously singing in heated unison, were truly a sight to behold. You could feel the group consciousness letting go of burdens, and opening up to something bigger than themselves. The Holy Spirit is the essence of God/Goddess, and it dwelled within every Baptist church service I attended, which was way too many to count.

One particular night, the preacher's eyes locked with mine, and he came toward me with a singular look of purpose etched on his face. He was on fire, with a mission to save the sinners. I was obviously first on his list, and I wasn't going to be able to get out of his way. Panic rose within me. What could I do? Where could I hide?

The next thing I remember is the weight of his large hand on the top of my little head. I felt as though my skull would be crushed and I began to shake uncontrollably, the way a rocket ship does before it takes off. Then I felt myself surrender to the experience, and I was filled with the most amazing bright white light. I felt it speed through my body, and back out the top of my head, in a split second. An immense feeling of joy from somewhere deep within spilled over encompassing my entire body. The vastness of the Holy Spirit had filled my vessel, and it was now overflowing beyond my container.

My sister said that after the preacher laid his hand upon my head and began to pray for my soul, I shook for a few minutes, fell to the floor, and began talking in tongues. Talking in tongues is when a person lets go, and an uncontrollable, unknown, language comes through in small consonants between chattering teeth. It felt totally weird, but I also felt ecstatically good. A powerful energy had coursed through me and I could barely hang on while I was speaking some foreign language. I had no control over what I was saying. Chattering away, I became separate from my physical body and viewed myself from above. After the exhilaration had run its course, I was gifted with a feeling of such peace and serenity.

After that night, I never sat in the front pew again. I was terrified of having another uncontrollable experience like that one. I didn't have any more experiences of either the Holy Ghost, or talking in tongues, ever again. However, I now had some new experiences that were just as powerful by almost dying. So many things changed for me when I woke up from my coma.

I became aware that my psychic abilities had turned on, and I didn't know how to turn them off. A nurse or janitor would come into my room, and I would instantly see their most intimate thoughts – where they were stuck in their life, and if they or a family member were in any kind of pain. Immediately reading them, I would then bring it up in a conversation, and together we would take a look at what wasn't working, and find solutions. Invariably, a lot of hugging and crying was beginning to go on in my hospital room, but people would then walk out with a glow around them.

Suddenly, my room had become a very popular place for staff to hang out. Since I didn't know how to turn off the psychic information that would zoom through my head, the psychic readings turned out to be exhausting for me in my weakened condition. I would have to ask the local psychic school about this problem. Maybe they knew the way to balance this psychic ability, and teach me how to turn it off when I wanted? I didn't like feeling out of control.

First Meeting With the Council

Flowing in and out of consciousness, I continued to remember the highlights of my childhood. An experience that opened me up to the possibility that the universe was way more diverse than what religion had led me to believe happened one afternoon when I was in the sixth grade. I was in assembly nervously awaiting my turn to be called up to the stage to represent my class and my school in the upcoming Peach Blossom Festival speech contest. It was an annual California competition. I really didn't want to go up there and be humiliated in front of the whole school if I made a mistake. I had been assigned, like all the other sixth-grade students, to choose a small story to read out loud in front of all our classmates.

I remember almost giving up on trying to find what to read. It was a stupid assignment. I didn't understand… what was the point? Our teacher took us to the school library. I was wandering aimlessly around, up and down the aisles of books, when all of a sudden; a small book with a green cover fell off the top shelf and landed on the floor directly in front of me, "bam." I picked up the book, read it quickly, and it made me laugh. The right book had chosen me, and I was so relieved.

I read that book to my classmates, and everyone laughed. I had always enjoyed making people laugh. I admired the simplicity of the story, and I thought I had done an "okay" job reciting it. I was surprised to find myself now waiting, as if forever, to be called to tell it again – only this time, in front of the entire school. I was terrified, excited, and all mixed up in one huge knot in the bottom of my stomach, and then it happened...

A few minutes before they were to call my name, a group of very tall beings dressed in white robes and hoods appeared out of thin air. I was the only one who saw and heard them. They stood slightly behind me and off toward my right shoulder. I could see them all, out of the corner of my right eye. I never saw their faces directly, as they were hidden by the large, open hoods of their gowns. I called them the Council, but I didn't know why. The Council communicated with me telepathically – mind to mind. I couldn't see their mouths move; I just knew that this was how they communicated.

The Council asked me the following question, "Would you like to someday in the distant future talk to thousands of people while on a large stage, and inspire them with your words, to give them hope? By doing this, you would have more joy than you could possibly imagine. Oh, and by the way, you will not get paid for doing it, if you accept. Would you be interested in doing this job?" I replied without thinking, "Yes! I would love to do that job, but my family is very poor and I would need to get paid for doing it."

I could feel the Council of beings was quite surprised by my request about getting paid. I suddenly felt that my request, or any request at all, was a highly unusual event, as it set off a kind of buzz of communication throughout the group. A twelve-year-old girl was questioning the Council? They nodded their hoods in agreement with each other, and then nodded in agreement to me. We had a deal. They laughed quietly among themselves. I didn't know at the time that the gift of joy they were offering me was and is priceless. They vanished as quickly as they had appeared.

This did not just all happen in my mind, because I could see them as clearly as I saw the girls sitting next to me that afternoon in the auditorium. Then my name was called. I walked quickly onto the stage and recited the story to the students and teachers – and mostly everyone laughed out loud.

The thunderous applause was a wonderful surprise. Discovering within me a sense of peace and pride in my abilities as a speaker sparked my self-worth and kindled love within for myself and for others. Little did I know that in the future, I would meet this Council again during another life-changing event, the night I almost died.

"A High Degree of Strangeness"

So exactly what led up to me laying in this hospital bed, recovering from the shock of almost dying? Being grateful to be alive and so many mixed emotions I was crying and laughing at the same time.

It was a typical cold early morning on December 4, 1989, in Sacramento, California. Awakened by the startling alarm sitting on the antique table next to my bed, I rolled over, smacked it hard with my hand, and begged for just five more minutes. Swinging my bare feet onto the cold, bare floor and standing up, I opened my eyes to see a white, wispy, etheric-looking cloud, engulfing my entire body, emanating from my head to my toes. It felt like an energetic force field of light.

My first thought was to go back to bed and get back up again, so hopefully the shocking white, wispy, etheric-looking cloud surrounding me might go away. I didn't have time to deal with anything strange and unfamiliar at the moment. Not giving it a second thought, I threw on my sweat pants, and sweatshirt, and went running down the hallway to turn on the water for a cup of the "Morning Goddess."

I had a busy schedule ahead of me that day. "Rise and shine," I sang to each of my children, to get up and get ready for school. That was our family tradition, as I always hated getting up in the morning and wanted to make school mornings for the kids as cheerful as possible.

It seemed like the white, wispy, etheric-looking cloud separated me from everything else. The surprise was that I was the only one who could see it. I asked my children if they saw anything around Momma, or if anything seemed odd? None of them noticed anything unusual, and we hurried through our daily morning rush to get to school.

My eyes were so sensitive to the light coming through the patio windows that I had to pull the curtains shut. That was unusual, because I loved the sun shining across the living room in the morning, when it left long, narrow beams of light spread across the walls and fine art paintings. Sounds were now intensified, and I found everything to be louder than normal. the white, wispy, etheric-looking cloud somehow was creating what I consider a "high degree of strangeness," meaning it needs further scientific study because it is so far out of the ordinary.

I called and asked my best friend, Cindy, if she could help drive the children to school for me because I was feeling really weird. It was unusual for me to ask for help, as I was used to doing everything alone. Cindy assured me that I didn't look weird as she walked through the front door, throwing her purse and keys on the kitchen table. Coming over to get a closer look at me, she mockingly teased, "I can sense that something isn't quite right here." She then made "koo-koo" motions with her fingers and rolled her large brown eyes. "Thanks." I sarcastically replied, and then we both laughed out loud.

Cindy, a metaphysician, agreed to read the energy and give me a healing. During the spontaneous reading, Cindy detected a force emanating around my body that, strangely, was stronger than my usual auric field. She was puzzled about its' nature, and thought it to be quite weird. Cindy knew me well, and she had given me dozens of readings and healings since we were both students at the local psychic school. Cindy was also a practicing midwife, and I valued her judgment tremendously. She suggested that we should go to the psychic school, and maybe they could help me, because it was definitely out of her expertise.

I looked at myself briefly in the mirror, and my body seemed to be full of white light. My skin appeared translucent, with a light blue hue underneath it. That certainly wasn't normal. What was that sound? It was the beating of my heart in my chest. I could feel and hear my heart beating, but the fact that I focused on it, instead of taking the beating for granted, seemed odd.

Cindy and I quickly dropped the children off at school and drove to the psychic school a few miles away. The director of the school would know what was going on and could help remove this "whatever it is" from me and get me back to normal. I had a lot of things I needed to get done, and neither Cindy nor I had time for all of this drama.

When we both stomped up the old, painted stairs of the grand Victorian house, situated discreetly in the downtown district, we were sure that everything would be healed quickly and that we could soon be on our way. We figured the director and staff of the school were master psychics, and had probably seen and dealt with just about everything. The head psychic in charge of healing that morning asked us to take a chair, ground ourselves, and run our energy.

A few minutes into it, I opened my eyes and saw the director looking at me with his glasses in hand, staring at me with quizzical eyes. I don't remember exactly what he said, but it went kind of like, "Barbara, your energy is so erratic, and you can't seem to control it. It's upsetting the energy of the entire school. You must leave immediately, and not come back until you get it together." I tried to explain that I was frightened, and that I needed a healing – but for reasons unknown to me, he just didn't want to hear anything I had to say.

There was a "high degree of strangeness" continuing to surround me, and I couldn't find anyone to help me. I had no control over it. What was happening to me? No one I knew – including the director, the veteran psychic teachers, or any of the psychic students – had a clue, and they all refused to help me. My regular doctor wouldn't be of any help, since she couldn't even see the white, wispy, etheric-looking cloud, and I certainly couldn't exactly explain my symptoms with any clear rationale.

Later that evening, the children were all ready for bed, dressed in their pajamas with squeaky-clean hair that was still a little damp and smelling of Herbal Essence shampoo. I kissed all of their heads, and told them to be good for the babysitter. As I drove to the women's spiritual open house, a thought ran through my mind that I shouldn't be driving because I was "out of it"… as though I'd had a few cocktails and just needed to lie down.

Darn it – I was running late, as usual. It seemed that as hard as I tried, I was usually fifteen minutes late, like clockwork. The white, wispy, etheric-looking cloud was still around me, but then I began to have difficulty breathing, as well. Yes, I definitely had a shortness of breath, and a tightening of the chest. These were the first signs of an asthma attack! Usually, I would just take a few puffs off of my albuterol inhaler, and within a few minutes, the asthma symptoms would subside. But, that was not the case now, as this "high degree of strangeness" kind of day continued into the evening.

Into The Void

I could not stop the asthma attack from happening, even with the aid of an inhaler that I carried in my purse at all times. My heart also began to pound like a locomotive gone off the tracks, and down the cliff, completely out of control. The pain was beginning to be unbearable, and I knew something was really wrong. I didn't think I could make it into the building where the women's open house was being held.

As I walked slowly toward the building where the open house was to be held, I stopped several times to hold onto cars in the parking lot to give me the support I needed to move forward. Maria, a woman whom I had seen several times at different psychic fairs, came running across the parking lot to help me. Being a psychic herself, she explained to me that she'd been told by her spirit guide to take her son's inhaler out of the glove box of her car, because someone would need it that night. So, she did. She said the moment she saw me, she knew I was the one that the inhaler was meant for.

By this time, I was hunched over due to lack of oxygen, and I could barely walk. Maria very gently and kindly helped me into the building. I entered the expansive room, which was filled with the loud voices of many excited women talking and laughing. They were busily taking off their scarves and coats and beginning to settle in for the evening's lecture. There was an air of excitement, for the evening's lecture was to be presented by the co-founder of the school. All the noise and chattering of the women's voices echoed waves of buzzing sounds into my ears, and I began to lose my balance.

Everything began to spin slowly, as I started losing control of my body. Suddenly the white, wispy etheric-looking cloud was closing in tightly around me. I felt a tremendous jolt of fear attack my entire body. I was gasping for air, but I could not breathe. An excruciating pain was thrusting into my chest, lungs, and upper back. It felt like a thousand hot knives had relentlessly forced their way into my heaving chest.

As I reached my maximum pain threshold, I cried out with all of my might, but the only thing that would come out of my mouth was a desperate whisper: "Can someone please stop this pain? Can somebody help me?" The pure intensity of the pain overtook me again and again, like crashing, cataclysmic waves upon a beach. The inhaler was definitely not working, and the frightening truth was that there was something terribly wrong happening. Terrified out of my mind, with my chest tightening up, I was just not getting enough air!

Mercifully, I blacked out. Against my will, Death had taken me into the void. I was released into the darkness of oblivion.

The Battle for My Soul

I was moved to the side of the room, where the women who were healers and psychics gathered to try and help me. The staff attempted to calm everyone down and continue the event. All of the women became very quiet. I was helped into a chair, since I didn't appear capable of sitting myself. My head and shoulders were slumped over my stomach. Still gasping for air, my body was no longer under my control. My face had become a light shade of green, translucent like that of a lizard's belly. My body had withered and did not have much energy in it. And that is when it happened.

My normal voice was gone, replaced by a male-sounding voice that spoke harshly and with authority. This sudden turn of events frightened the women. I had suddenly appeared to be ancient. The commanding being, channeling through me, informed the women that he was from Egypt, a long time ago. The ancient being channeled his energy through my body, so much so that he had successfully kicked me completely out. I was totally unaware that my body was hijacked.

He informed the women in a raspy voice that he would not allow me to live, because I had information that was not allowed at this time. When was the right time? What information was not allowed? The scene had become quite seriously life threatening. If I could have seen myself, I am sure I would have been thoroughly embarrassed and mortified. A thousand apologies would have not been enough.

Barbara Jean Lindsey

The ancient Egyptian being continued to threaten the women, and screamed, "I am going to kill her, now! This is what I am going to do." He then follows through on his threat. He proceeded to collapse both of my lungs! Someone had called for an ambulance, and it arrived just in time.

It would be over five years before I would get enough courage to get copies of my hospital records. It took several more years to be able to watch on television someone being defibrillated without feeling panic myself. The scene of the doctor putting the electrical pads onto someone's heart, and saying the word "Clear!" was enough to send me into immediate, intense fear and anxiety.

A significant incident occurred during the night's dramatic events. Cindy told me that the psychic doing the evening's channeling had received some extraordinary information. Another ancient being, who said his name was Thor, showed up during my battle with the ancient Egyptian and fought him with all of his might for my life. Fortunately for me he quickly won. What did they use for fighting, swords and lightning bolts?

Now I know this all sounds very strange, and I am the first to agree, but these events really happened, and I am not exaggerating. In fact, I am trying my very best not to embellish or delete anything that I was told occurred that night. I assure you I am fiercely dedicated to the truth. You are welcome to your opinion. I would appreciate it if you would hear me out before you make up your mind.

That night's events were seen and experienced by about fifty women, most of who were psychic students or psychic teachers. Each and every one of them had a valid experience, whatever that might be. I am retelling the story as it was told to me, in the best way that I know, even if it does seem "out of this world."

Coincidence

At the hospital that fateful night, the pulmonary specialist just happened to be there when I was admitted to the emergency room. Forgetting something, he had just stopped by for a minute to pick it up. On his way out the door, a nurse urgently asked him if he could take a quick look at a thirty-seven-year-old woman who had just been admitted, and was in severe danger of dying.

The specialist found me to be in extreme distress. All the doctors, nurses and staff were doing everything they possibly could to keep me alive.

My medical chart stated, *"The specialist reverted to hand ventilation to maximize ventilation, as by this time, even with the endotracheal tube, the patient's PCO2 was 99 torque, PH 7.02 and ventilator therapy at that juncture had brought the PCO2 down only to 68, PH 7.20 in extreme distress and at the point of appearing in severe danger of expiring and obviously continues to be at death's door at this point."* The specialist stabilized me as best he could, and the rest was up to God/Goddess.

I was transferred from emergency into the intensive care unit. The specialist advised Cindy, that my family should be notified as soon as possible. They were told that if I did survive the trauma, they could say goodbye to the Barbara they once knew, because they were sure permanent damage had occurred due to lack of oxygen to my brain. They just didn't know to what extent.

I was rapidly deteriorating obviously at death's door, and the specialist realized my condition merited extreme measures. Since I was undoubtedly about to die any moment, he delivered several exceptionally high therapeutic doses of electrical shock to my heart with a defibrillator. The specialist said he was very surprised that I survived at all. The puzzling fact that I was still alive was truly a medical wonder. Even though death was imminent that night, I was given a second chance to live and tell the story thanks, in part to the "coincidence," (which I really don't believe in of the specialist just happening to be there.)

My Physical Body

My body was being monitored, and the machines were breathing for me. All of my vital signs were beginning to stabilize. I continue to give thanks to the good graces of the ambulance driver and emergency team, Western medicine, the caring,intelligent doctors, nurses and all of the hospital staff, for doing such an extraordinary job in helping to save my life that night.

I give thanks to my family, friends, and fellow psychic students and teachers, who continued to pray, and who watched me psychically, physically, and consciously separate from my body. Cindy, told me later that she and many other psychics saw me after the battle ended, in the heavens celebrating, and joyously unaware of my Earth body and its' fragile condition.

After the ambulance left with me, the psychic school set up a twenty-four-hour prayer vigil. Many psychics participated, not only in my hometown, but throughout the California network as well. I feel that the power of the prayers of so many people helped keep my body illuminated with white light so that the communication between my body and soul stayed vitally strong. The prayers were being heard and my body was safe. I, as a spirit, was set free to investigate the great mysteries of life and the illusions of death... and entered the Afterlife.

The Afterlife

I did not go into
A tunnel of light
I became the light
I am full
I am whole
I am complete
I did not review my life
I am life
I am entirely
In the moment
The creator and I
Are one
Evolving, changing, moving
A spiraling of death and rebirth
Again and again and again…
I am simple
I am highly intellectual
All
At the same time
I am one
With everything
It and I
Are a
Blissful union
Timeless love
And
Magnificent Beauty
I am

More alive
Now than
I have
Ever been
Before
In this
Afterlife

What It Feels Like To Be Dead

While my physical body, unknown to me at the time, was being taken care of by the emergency medical team as best they could, I, as a spirit, immediately transitioned from the intense space of profound pain and suffering into the complete awareness of absolutely no pain whatsoever. Instantly, like the snap of my fingers, I was set free.

I found myself still alive surrounded by nothingness, with no definition of myself whatsoever. My body had completely disappeared. Yes, that is right, my body had completely disappeared. Yet, I still existed. *How is that possible, I thought?* I am still existing, but I don't have a body! I could see, just as if I had eyes, but I didn't see my body: that is, no hands, fingers, legs, feet, face or hair. My body did not exist! Yet, I feel totally alive, the way I did when I had a body.

I had no beginning and no end. I was everything and nothing. I had complete awareness of my senses. I was floating in a sea of warm, liquid, love light – deliciously alive water, like a warm sea on a tropical island with a slight breeze. The gentle waves were dark, and yet so light at the same time. I was surrounded by love in every aspect of my being. Being gently rocked by small waves of buoyant love caresses, I let go and let go and let go.

The source was sending soothing, sweet murmurs of loving tones into my ears. I was ultimately comfortable, and at last, I felt such relief. I was home. I felt so alert and aware, but most of all free from all of my body's pain and suffering.

I was melted into the Light... into the Light... into the Light... into the Holy of Holies... into the whole, the cosmic void... into the warmth... the exquisite magnificence of the mystery of the love force. I was floating in the liquid magma of life... internal, creating and recreating itself, all eternal love, ever flowing and never ending.

I felt the beauty and eternal bliss of the opening of my heart into my whole being, which is I, which is you, which is the future, the present and the entire accumulated past of every thought, idea and desire. I was melted... I had no beginning and no end. I was just one in the complete wholeness of love, the Creator of all that is. All of my emotional feelings were so light and effervescent. I continued floating in a pool of warmth and light, turned a golden, delicious color filled with sparkles of joy and tenderness.

It was like being a baby again, held in my mother's loving and safe arms. I was floating... I was floating. I don't know for how long. Since this love is timeless and I knew I was from this love, I didn't ever want to leave. It was I and I am it, in complete totality; not a piece was missing. I was whole and completely perfect. The joy in and around me was beyond my human experience of complete and utter ecstasy. I continued to float and be...be...be... I was exalted, honored, and loved unconditionally through every thread of my being. I am... I am... I am... I am love... love... love...love... love... l o v e. I had become one with everything.

The Space Ship

Then, in what seemed like a split second in time, I was on a spaceship. How did I know it was a spaceship? It appeared to look similar to the spaceships I had seen in the 1970's classic movies, like "Star Wars" and "Close Encounters of the Third Kind," those being my only reference points at the time.

This spaceship had rounded corners, slick smooth surfaces, filtered soft lighting in the top of the wall, no switches, no lamps, and a high rounded ceiling. Not a square angle to be seen anywhere. The air was filtered with a cool, clean, almost sweet smell. Everything was so very clean and shiny, but soft at the same time.

The spaceship seemed to be running on its own intelligence somehow, like "HAL" in the Stanley Kubrick movie, "2001: A Space Odyssey." What was happening to me? Did my imagination just get the best of me? Am I more than just a "lil bit touched," and have I gone way down into Alice in Wonderland's rabbit hole? Was this some secret, 3-D government Special Ops program running in my brain?

I found myself sitting in a slightly reclined position, quite comfortable, with my arms supported by the padded arms of a tall-legged chair, and with my feet suspended slightly upward by an attached cushion, La-Z-Boy style. It looked like a cool, modern type dentist chair without the equipment. The materials were in a glossy mahogany finish, with the cushions in slick, cocoa-brown fabric. It was a large, circular room, and I was situated directly in the middle with nothing around me.

Directly in front of me, about three feet away, stood the tallest being I had ever seen: well over eight feet tall, maybe taller. He gave the appearance of being masculine. Not that he had any noted outward appearance of a male, he just felt like one. Don't ask me how; I simply knew he was a male being. There were no sexual energies exchanged, much more like an indeterminate sex.

I got the distinct feeling that he and the spaceship weren't from around here – I mean Earth, that is. I didn't freak out or anything. It was just a matter of fact, and I was dealing quite nicely, considering that I was on a spaceship in the middle of nowhere and communicating with an extraterrestrial being.

Feeling completely focused, and fully present to absorb and learn as much as I possibly could from the experience, I was suddenly more alive now in this moment than I had ever been on Earth. Not in a dream-like state at all: quite the opposite. I was fully conscious, and completely aware of everything that was happening to me.

I could feel my body, but I couldn't quite see my body. I could feel its weight and its definition, as though I was the same size that I was on Earth. I still had the same face, arms, legs, feet and hair, but for some reason, I could not see it with my eyes. However, I could see everything around me in sharp focus. It was an odd sensation, but not alarming. I was still me, a thirty-seven-year-old female from Planet Earth.

The being stood erect. He had large, square shoulders and long, beautiful, artistic Leonardo Da Vinci-like hands, including four slender fingers and a thumb on each: quite human looking. The large hood attached to his robe cast a dark shadow that blocked me from ever seeing his face. In place of where his face would have been was nothing but utter darkness. For some reason, this did not frighten me, but was just taken as fact, with no emotional reactions on my part.

A white robe extended from the being's shoulders to the floor in a flowing fashion. I could not see his feet. His robe was simple and elegant, without decoration; trimmed with a high, rounded, white collar with long, flowing, open sleeves. His robe appeared to have been made from a natural cotton or raw silk fabric. It hung loosely on his body, and he moved with comfort and agility as he came closer towards me.

The tall being was very elegant and masterful in his countenance. All of his gestures were graceful and non-threatening. He gave me the feeling of great intelligence and sophistication. I immediately felt great peace and comfort in his presence. He seemed familiar, like an old and dear friend, like a guardian, an ancient grandfather, or a Grand Master. He reassured me that he had my best interest at heart.

He began to communicate to me telepathically. I could feel and understand his thoughts. He communicated to me heart to heart, being to being, direct and clear and with great speed. It was so much fun! It was like a thousand words expressed in a moment, as in the way fine art communicates. I had never conversed telepathically before that I could remember, and I really liked it much better than the way we talked on Earth, which now seemed so much more primitive. I was relaxed, and not feeling threatened in anyway whatsoever.

The being gave a slight bow, and then he told me that he was honored to be the main communicator and translator for a group of beings that I had not met yet. I understand now that I am to call him the Guardian. He turned and pointed to the back of the spaceship and waved his hand, gesturing to a darkened rectangular section to his right.

All of a sudden as if a light had switched on, there they were. I could see about ten beings, but I don't know exactly how many there were. It was almost as if they were connected by a portal that resonated at a different time and space through a large clear wall. The Guardian introduced them, and I called them the Council. I don't know why.

The Guardian was the only communicator between the Council and myself. I felt that it was part of the Guardian's job to keep me comfortable, relaxed, and awake, to get the transmission from the Council.

The Council was of the same appearance as the Guardian, in that their presence seemed to be sophisticated, highly intelligent, and very gentle. Each Council member had his own unique expression of presence. Not so much physically, but with personality differences in their movements, body posture and gestures. I can't remember exactly what they looked like, except that some sat up taller than the others, and some were heavier than others. I was unable to see any of their faces. They all wore the same exact matching hooded white robes as the Guardian.

I felt rather like I was on display for viewing, much like animals must feel in a zoo, with people watching their every move. I wasn't afraid ever; I was just trying to figure the whole scene out.

The Council was sitting. I never saw the backs of whatever they were sitting on. Strangely, I could see a mahogany conference room table in front of a glass wall. That glass wall separated the Council from me. I thought how the mahogany table looked so out of place in such a modern and pristine environment. Where were all the matching chairs? Was it there to make me feel more at home? It just seemed odd.

In the beginning, when we were first introduced, the Council was all sitting facing me. At other times they would all be standing in from of the large glass wall, staring directly at me in unison.

The Council of beings would telepathically communicate with each other, sometimes passionately. Some members would stand up, and then sit down, then another member would stand up, telepath, and sit down as if in a heated discussion. The Council would come to a final agreement, and then transmit collectively to the Guardian their agreed communication for me.

Upon receiving the information from the Council, the Guardian would translate and relay it directly to me. The process proceeded quickly, and the exchange of information was not only telepathic but also presented to me visually and experientially. I don't know how long the Council and I exchanged information. It seemed like forever, and then again, it was like a blink of an eye, all at the same time.

Cosmic Mother Earth

A large, round window appeared slightly to my right; about the size of the typical movie screen you see when you visit your local movie theater. The window was surrounded by a bright white trim. Projected onto the round screen was the image of our Planet Earth, rotating among the other planets in our galaxy. The image of the Earth began to move closer and closer, and faster and faster, toward me. I had all of my focus on the Planet Earth.

The Earth jumped right into my space, up close and personal – or I jumped into the Earth, I wasn't sure which one was which. I felt that I had completely merged with the Earth … no boundaries. I could feel the oneness of the Earth and myself, I and the Earth. I could feel the aliveness of the Earth. She was a living entity, because I could feel and hear the sound of her heartbeat.

Then my heartbeat and the heartbeat of Mother Earth were the same. I became one with Mother Earth. A slow, rhythmic beat like that of a Native American drum, and the tone of a guttural Tibetan chant, united with my own heartbeat. My breathing slowed down to meet the rhythm of the Earth. We harmonized and synchronized our hearts.

I was told, in my mind, how valuable our Mother Earth was to herself and all of her people. The whole existence of the star system could be thrown out of balance without her beauty and magnificence. I must protect her. We must help protect her. There would come a time, sooner rather than later, where the exploitation of her resources must come to an end. Balance is crucial.

Sobbing uncontrollably, I had not understood the magnitude of the beauty and importance of our Mother Earth. Our Earth was a magical blue planet, very much alive, and strategically placed in the whole brilliance of the entirety of the Cosmos. I had taken her for granted. I was not aware; I was single minded, and not conscious of my connection and relationship to our planet. I suddenly recognized her profound and natural love, her nurturing of all life.

In that moment of self-realization, I became one with our planet, and aware of our galactic heritage. The Earth, our galactic brothers and sisters, and we humans, are all one collective consciousness. What one does affects the other. I became awakened to an amazing relationship with our Mother Earth and her omnipotent power and beauty. I became aware that if I am out of balance, then she is out of balance.

Green

Coming back from the vision of the Earth rotating intimately with my mind, body and soul, I then flew upward out of my seat with my Guardian on my left side. We immediately soared high in the air, completely through the spaceship ceiling like boundless eagles, with grace and speed, out into nothingness.

Flying for a short distance I could suddenly see the ground below, as if from the height of an airplane passenger's viewpoint. Abundant green mountains and valleys appeared as far as the eye could see.

It was like a continuous kaleidoscope of amazingly soft, velvety mounds, small hills, mountain scapes and varied depths of valleys, all covered in mossy textures and intense shades of green. So many ranges and tones of green from the lightest celery to the intense emeralds, unlike anything I could have ever imagined. I really didn't see any people or buildings, just a continuous, gentle flight over the wondrous Technicolor Green mountains and valleys. Observing the forest's beauty and splendor, it was truly beyond earthly description.

Feelings of such joy burst from my heart while bathing in and completely absorbing Green in every aspect. I had been re-sparked with the primordial knowing of the essence of Green deep in my soul. It was as if, Green had never left me. I could feel and breathe Green again! Like the excitement of childhood memories of coming home after being gone for a long time. Green was dynamic and juicy. Green was deep and lush. I felt Green's fullness of being alive. Don't ask me how! This was my experience of Green. I felt honored to be in such splendor.

The green mountains and valleys were nurturing my heart and soul. I was part of the green of nature. Green was a part of me. I knew green. Green knew me. The color of green was deep and wise and ancient, and existed within me. Green was timeless and free. The glorious salutation of green awakened my senses. It was so very cool it blew my mind. I gave thanks. Green healed my heart and re-ignited my soul.

The Watchers

Seeing the Guardian to my left side, I sensed the presence of other guides, whom I could not see, hovering around me. They gently and ever so lightly, in a flash of an instant, transported me to a new vision and experience. As my feet touched the ground, I observed in the near distance a vista filled with a breathtakingly beautiful view of one single, gigantic circle of perfect, colossal, white columns, precisely set apart in equal distances, similar to that of a historic Greek temple.

At the base of the temple was a flight of stairs, filled with soft white light appearing from nowhere. As I had the thought I wanted to go there, I was instantaneously at the base of the stairs. Immediately I climbed up the alabaster stone stairs until I landed at the top.

What came to my view was breathtakingly majestic. Not only could I see the colossal columns, but behind and in between them sparkled the backdrop of millions of stars within a deep vastness of space. It looked to me as though this ancient temple existed somewhere in the middle of the boundless Cosmos, floating in timeless space. Exactly in the center of the circle of columns stood yet another perfect circle of tall, square-shouldered beings, holding hands.

They were all dressed the same, in white ceremonial robes with attached hoods that hid their faces, exactly the same like that as the Guardian. They introduced themselves to me, telepathically, as simply, "The Watchers."

In focused union, the Watchers were all peering over a monumental, round, white, cauldron-looking vessel, which was mounted on a matching white pedestal column, placed directly in the center of the circular columns. The cauldron was filled with still, dark, translucent liquid that looked a lot like seawater with reflected moonlight on a dark night. The white misty vapors were gently shooting up from within and around the water, filling the surrounding space with a gentle white fog in the darkness.

The Watchers said they had missed me, and expressed kindness and affection. No words were exchanged. I had indeed become one with the group almost immediately – it was as if they had been expecting me. The union of the Watchers continued to stare into the dark waters, and through the vapors, with great intention and focus.

As I moved closer, two beings opened the circle so that I could join hands and continue the connection. As I began to lose my sense of self, separate and isolated from the group, I emerged into the Watchers' consciousness and became linked with all present. We instantly became one, together in mind, spirit and focus.

After meditating upon the vessel for a short time, the image of Planet Earth appeared, from nowhere, in the direct center. The small hologram of the Earth was floating in a circular rotation, hovering slightly above the vapor mist. The Watchers told me that it was their privilege to observe Earth, and see that she is continually safe from total destruction.

They possessed such omnipresent love and respect for our beautiful blue planet. It seemed to be such a simple gathering, and yet the reality of its existence was profound. The powerful energy emanating from the watchers was a pure, radiant, pearl essence of white color. I was hanging out with white lightning, and I was becoming radiant. I was feeling their love, and it felt sincere and ecstatic. The Watchers reminded me that I could return to this celestial mountain whenever I so desired. I felt honored and relieved that such magnificent beings of light were in alignment with our beautiful Planet Earth.

Galactic Gala

I was the only human I could see in any direction. My guardian and I had appeared in the front of an entrance to a great and wondrous opening to a classic grand ballroom, Victorian style, only austere and modern. To each side, tall, multi-colored plants appeared to be dusted with a light-golden, sparkling finish. As we proceeded down the hallway, we came to the top of a long, sweeping staircase, which had a cascading view of the entire scene. It was a party or gala of some sort. I wasn't sure what it was exactly, because it was so odd. It took some getting used to.

There was an extreme array of countless beings of different shapes, colors and sizes. There were fat beings, thin beings, soft beings, tall beings, short beings, furry beings, pink beings, serious beings, and jovial beings, the likes of which I had never seen before. There was much talking, laughing, varied hand shaking, hugs, kisses and downright friendly greetings exchanged repeatedly with everyone, only in a more dignified, professional manner.

I didn't see any food being served, but I did notice trays of delicious-looking, primary-colored drinks in thin, clear tubes, being served on a clear tray by a waiter with white gloves. I noticed that, for some reason, my Guardian stayed close to my side and maneuvered his way through the crowd. It was as if I had just landed smack dab in the middle of a colossal social gathering of dignitaries from different worlds.

One thing that was apparent was they all had the ability to communicate in many different languages. Each being had a medal or ribbon, which represented his/her/its' home. I couldn't understand any of the languages; they were all alien to me. Some were talking telepathically, and some were having conversations out loud, as well. The sounds of the background music were on the jazzy side, but I never saw who or what was playing. The air was as an elixir, light and sweet.

The structure where the festivity took place reminded me for some reason of an old Victorian parlor, with brightly painted white wooden beams and huge, glass-paneled doors and windows, only greatly magnified, minus the rugs and furniture. The ceiling of the solarium must have been at least a hundred feet high. I could see the stars through the glass ceiling, which was partly open. There was coolness, coupled with excitement, in the crisp air. I was in the middle of an "ambassador" party. An ambassador party, I was told by my Guardian, was where beings who had not seen each other in a while came to talk, exchange ideas, find solutions to problems, and honor their connections of what they had in common for the good of all who were present and the planets they represented.

My Guardian introduced me to many ambassadors. I felt very well received. Everyone was quite polite. It seemed customary to make a slight bow, and then be introduced. I still could not see my body. When I looked down at myself, I could see an ethereal outline but with no real definition. I was beginning to lose my sense of physical self, and communicating in a more important way: spirit-to-spirit. The boundary of viewing myself only as a physical body was elevated to perceiving myself as a timeless spirit.

The greetings were warm, and full of sincerity. Everyone was patient. There seemed to be an excitement in the air. They seemed to be somewhat quizzical about my appearance, at least that is the feeling that I received. The Ambassadors could apparently see me without any problem; I just couldn't really see myself. Many told me telepathically that they enjoyed my smile very much. I could feel myself smiling. I had become part of a social association of galactic ambassadors, fiercely dedicated to honoring truth and freedom of all species everywhere. Feeling so humbled to be in the presence of such high level beings, I wondered what the heck was I doing there?

Every good party has an ending. All too soon, it became time to leave. And I was just beginning to relax and get the hang of things. I did not want to go. Learning about communicating spirit to spirit, and heart to heart, was truly a worthwhile course of study, and I had so much to learn. Making my last gestures of gratitude, I bowed slightly and took a final sweeping glance of all the dignitaries present. I tried to lock the extraordinary events into my memory so that it would never be forgotten.

Goddesses & Angels

I was suddenly whisked away once again by my Guardian, up and up, higher and higher, lighter and lighter, brighter and brighter, into the veils of the white mists of nothingness. Surrounded by an infinite circle of faded blackness, I found myself floating, with no bottom, no top and no sides. With my hair flowing, I was gently swayed from side to side, as I was completely surrounded by an endlessly dark void. Somewhere from above there was an intense, bright, white light radiating. Without ground below me, I was danced, swirled around and around like a whirling dervish in the midnight air. I spiraled up and up, around and around. Flying limitlessly, unbridled into the mightiest force in the entire universe – the power of love.

Many Angels appeared and surrounded me, and we played, laughed, and danced as they sang joyful tones. Some chanted and played harps and flutes. The Angels appeared in the female Goddess form with flowing gowns of various jewel tones, from the deepest emeralds to the most fiery sunburst oranges to the deepest depths of lapis blue and transcendent turquoises. Their long, flowing hair was adorned with flowers, accented with intricately crafted necklaces and earrings of pearls and gems, elegantly set in enameled precious metals. Some playfully held each other's hands, like children. The Angels appeared very innocent, natural, and uninhibited.

I had read that real Angels did not have gender. Like beautiful John William Waterhouse paintings of classic, pre-Raphaelite ladies; these Angels glowed from within. They sang tones like queenly sirens of the deepest oceans. What was odd was that I couldn't hear any words, only high-pitched tones in glorious, soprano harmonies.

They nodded for me to join them in singing. I was shy and didn't think I had a voice. After much coaxing from the Angels, my voice opened gently at first, and I healed with each note I sang. Because as I continued to sing, I found my tone, and it was deeper than I expected. We then sang our hearts out together in unison, in a circle, while floating in misty white clouds. I was filled with beauty and love. Their communication with me was telepathic. The singing was not heard by my ears, but understood and emblazoned upon my heart.

I was singing, but I couldn't hear it with my normal hearing abilities because I had become the singing. I was ecstatic. It was better than taking the middle bite out of a chilled, organic, homegrown watermelon on a hot summer's day. I saw the experience in Technicolor, and heard it with added celestial toning. The feelings were sweet and delicious. I soaked it all up, every delicious drop. I freely flew with Angels and joyously sang out with all of my heart. There were such sensations of joy beyond my wildest imagination. I was as a child again.

My heart burst forth uninhibited, and it flowed over and out like an endless river into the radiant, loving atmosphere. The magnificent presence of the angels flooded my soul, and every cell of my being, with love. Inspiration and hope suddenly became my new best friends, protecting my future aspirations.

Re-inspired by love, I am to dream a new dream, many new dreams, into infinity and beyond. It would be up to me to make all of my dreams come true.

The Gift of the White Light

Without warning the Guardian appeared once again and gazed at me. I stared into and through the dark void of a faceless spaceman wrapped in his white hood, as I still couldn't see a face. I definitely felt his immediate presence. The Council was nowhere to be seen. Suddenly, I got the hint, it was time to go home. "Oh, no!" I shouted, telepathically, I didn't want to go back home. I was having the most fantastically awesome time. Every experience had been healing, enlightening, or stimulating – fun, and euphoric. I wasn't ready to go home yet. The Guardian explained telepathically that it was now time for me to go back to my beloved children and my precious life. I had important work to do.

I began to think of my three children, who needed me. However, my first thought was that they would be fine without me. The children would learn their lessons, grow, change, and be guided into their unique destinies. Those thoughts were so unlike me, before I died. Beginning to have rebellious thoughts of not leaving this celestial place, I began to really remember that they were not "the" children, but "my" children, and I was reconnected to my profound love. The mother's love that I felt for all three of my children, which was a deep, timeless devotion that rang true in my heart and soul.

My children would be devastated without me in their lives. They had experienced so much confusion and sorrow with the divorce; they needed me to help them lovingly heal and recover.

In that split second of time of all knowing, I was re-united with that power of my love and spiritual bond with my children. My children needed me. I desired, more than anything, to be with my children. My beautiful children were waiting for me. I had to get home immediately.

As I recognized my true desire to be reunited with my children, I instantly spiraled down, down, down – and I found myself floating near the ceiling above a body lying sideways in a small hospital bed. The body was that of a woman with short legs, and long, dark, straight hair, sleeping in a wrinkled hospital gown. My best friend, Cindy, was sitting in a chair next to the bed, deep in meditation and prayer. What was she doing there in the hospital? Cindy looked like a guardian angel, radiating peace and well-being, as she sat with her eyes closed and a slight, uplifted smile, much like the pictures you see of the Buddha in meditation.

Once again, I scanned the body lying in the bed from head to toe, but still didn't quite get what was going on. I was somewhat confused. I had been having such a tremendous time without a body. Who was that person lying in that hospital bed, and what was I doing, floating here on the ceiling of this hospital room. In shock, I looked for the Guardian there and he was by my side. Observing my surroundings, I felt disconnected from it all.

As a spirit, I had become completely free of the sensations of the body, and I had no sense of pain, fear, or panic. Who was that person lying in the bed? There was no sense of ownership or excitement; it was merely a logical fact that a female body was in a hospital bed below me. I didn't recognize myself at all for a few moments.

Then I remembered that it was me, Barbara, lying in that hospital bed and I knew it was now time to transition back into my body. Suddenly a sense of urgency occurred to quickly return to my body. Yet, I was resistant. It was all happening too fast! Panic set in. I reached out to the Guardian and asked, "What do I do if I ever need help?" It was appallingly apparent that I was definitely going to need some serious help in my Earth body!

My Guardian took my hand into his, and quietly replied, "All you ever have to do, Barbara, is call in the White Light, and it will always be there for you." The Guardian had responded lovingly in such a calming, reassuring way. "Call in the White Light. Call in the White Light? That is it? That is all I need to do? That is all the help I am going to get, after all that I had just been through?" I couldn't believe it!

I thought the Guardian was kidding me. He chuckled quietly. I didn't think it was very funny. "Don't I get something real and substantial to take home with me?" I begged. I thought to myself, couldn't I get something tangible like a "Get Out of Jail Free Card," a secret handshake or an invincible power? I only had to ask for "White Light" if I needed something? In case of emergency, simply bring in the white light?

I still couldn't believe it. I was actually angry about the idea of bringing in "the White Light." In that moment, White Light seemed like such a small gift, almost like a joke, in comparison to everything I had experienced with the Guardian in the Afterlife.

What I might experience going back to an Earth body seemed shocking and extremely harsh compared to the euphoric state I had quickly become accustomed to without a body. I became resistant, totally fearful, through and through. Not about my body, but about having to go back into it alone… the way it was before my NDE… as if none of this had ever happened.

I wasn't happy about the extreme situation I was thrown into, seemingly without a care from the Guardian. I threw a fit, a small tantrum, like a demanding child who wasn't getting what she wanted. "I don't want to go back!" I cried telepathically. It wasn't fair. Defiantly, I stomped my foot and crossed my arms over my chest and tried to puff myself up with the best defensive stance that I could muster. Standing my ground, I was in shock and bewildered.

Then I remembered my children, and once again my heart melted. That is all that it took and I was ready to go back and return to my previous life. Hopefully, I would be able to bring in the White Light in any emergency situation. This would be all the assistance I required for the transition from existing as consciousness without a body in the Afterlife, to the daily routine of an ordinary life back on Earth. Like the flip of a coin, I was on the other side of fear, and eager to go back to the body I called home for thirty-seven years.

My Mission

Just as I began to descend into my body, my Guardian interrupted my focus and asked me to stop for a moment. As I hesitated, we both floated gently in unison above my physical self. He disclosed to me that I had a mission to carry out on Earth if I wanted to accept it. The Guardian further explained that I, of course, had free will to choose. Without thinking, I immediately replied with a resounding, "Yes! I will accept the mission." What was the actual mission was, I couldn't tell you. My Guardian then stated in a very formal and dignified manner, "Your mission is to be an Ambassador."

Smiling, at the Guardian, I thought with delight, I am going to be an Ambassador. That sounds really cool! I was over the moon. Then, I asked, "What is an Ambassador?" My Guardian never had a chance to answer. As I abruptly floated back down toward my body, I briefly glanced back. The Guardian had completely disappeared out of my sight.

Skin Dressing

I continued to hover gently a few feet above my body. Looking down this time, I admired its' natural beauty and inherent power. Laughing quietly to myself, I thought I didn't look that bad. It could be a lot worse. But I didn't look that fabulous either. I looked puffy.

Reassuring myself that everything was going to be okay, I reconsidered that having a body might, not be a bad idea after all. Being thankful for the gift of experiencing life in a woman's body had possibilities. I then began the transformation from spirit into becoming one with my physical form.

Quickly passing through several layers of my compressed body, I became aware of how dense it was. While, as spirit, I was so light. Suddenly I was catapulted into experiencing my body's excruciating pain. It was like I was rebirthing myself, and I was riding the intensity of the process. I couldn't go back. I couldn't escape. I couldn't go around… the only option I had was to ride it through to the other side, and surrender.

As I descended, deeper into the body itself, I continued enduring jolts of excruciating pain, and it became more and more intense. Continuing to suffer multiple electrical shocks, and waves of extreme anguish and agony, I didn't think I could take much more.

My body was so intensely heavy, and cumbersome. The Native Americans describe the physical body as one's "skin dressing." It felt exactly as though I was climbing into a new skin and trying it on for size. I didn't know where anything was, and I had to explore how it all worked as I continued the process of acclimating. I suffered through the pain until it broke... and then magically, I was set free of agony's hold.

As the White Light of spirit, I transitioned back, into every aspect of my body fully, – and I completely reclaimed it. White Light filled the top of my head and face, and it moved throughout me; from head to toes, including all cells, blood, tissues, bones, muscles, skin and hair. The White Light poured through my entire body, like a shining star filling every inch at lightning speed.

I then began to try my body on for size. I realigned with my spine first, beginning at the base, and working up to the crown of my head, relaxing everything into its proper place.

As I reclaimed the full ownership of my body, I began to sink into each layer. As I did the density of it lessened and lessened. When I reached the top of my head, the original density had become much lighter and brighter.

There became no separation between my lightness of being and the connection to the wholeness of my physical body. I was glowing. After fully reclaiming or rebirthing back into my body, I, with complete consciousness, took my first breath, filled with White Light. I sat straight up, in the hospital bed, and opened my green eyes once again. I was back... and boy, was I hungry!

Acclimation

After spending ten days in the hospital, I was finally released to go back to work, to my children, my family, and my home. I was given a clean bill of health by the medical professionals, and reminded to take my daily asthma medication. They declared me a walking, talking, medical miracle. I had faced death, kicked down her doors, met a Guardian, had visions, accepted being an "Ambassador," and returned to live and tell the story.

Yes, I was lucky. Going home to my children, family, and friends who loved me was one of life's sweetest gifts. I would continue my healing process not only physically, but I would have to integrate all that I had learned from my near death experience into my everyday life. It was like trying to pour a gallon of pure water into a thimble and make it work. How do I do that?

I experienced a quietness within myself that was deep, and peaceful. I required time to do nothing, be nothing, and still hang out with spirit between the worlds. Life seemed to be moving at a much faster rate than I remembered. There were fast cars, fast food, conveniences to save time – and everyone seemed to be in a big hurry because time was running out. It seemed that the faster everything appeared to be going, the more I needed to be alone and quiet. I needed to slow down... way down into a quiet solitude to survive, and not lose myself.

After the NDE, I discovered I didn't talk as much and listened more. I was not in a hurry anymore. I had slowed down not only inside, but also outside. I had found a profound peace, and a new spiritual center to enjoy life. I had acquired a sense of thankfulness and gratefulness for the gift of life. I had become ultra sensitive to sunlight, and I had to wear sunglasses. I saw colors differently than I had before I spent time in the Afterlife. Colors seemed to be more sharp, vivid and alive – almost animated. I had become acutely more sensitive to pain and suffering.

Wrapping My Brain Around It

The International Association for Near-Death Studies (IANDS) is an organization for researching and disseminating information on the phenomena of the near death experience (NDE). According to IANDS, adjusting to the aftereffects takes time. "The first three years tend to be the most confusing, almost as if the individual isn't fully back."

My doctors reassured me that I would go back to my normal routine and have a normal life, as soon as I was released from the hospital. I thought to myself that they don't have a clue about what had just happened to me. My physical body might have come through the NDE just fine, but who I was before I died would never be the same.

My NDE was all that I would talk about to anyone who would listen. It seemed as though talking would help put everything into order. All of my close friends were interested in listening about it, but I found that words to express the NDE for myself, personally and intimately were hard to find.

Becoming very confident in my new ideas about awareness, I could easily set up a pulpit on the downtown street corner, and preach about death as an incredible doorway to a new life. Sharing how valuable our experience is here on Earth... – and how our Earth needs our awareness to help her heal. I could go on a rampage of the possibilities of self-destruction, Mother Earth's ruin, and an awareness of our place as humans in the intergalactic big picture. That was the new NDE Barbara, who now had the global perspective, and who had become a warrior of consciousness to grow, change and evolve.

Then there was the contented, joyous Barbara who just wanted to stay home, take care of her kids, garden, swim, and enjoy life's daily gifts, just as she had before the NDE. I was trying to make some sense out of something that felt so big, so enormous, that I had difficulty wrapping my brain around it.

I thought, "Holy crap, what just happened?" What just happened was that my complete, entire perspective of who I was and what my life was all about had just completely transformed, one hundred percent. My life had been irrevocably changed forever.

How does one grasp so much change, in such a short time, without going crazy? My answer is, without a doubt, the love of my children. I had three children whom I adored, and loved more than life itself. The most important thing for me was being a good momma to my kids. The children grounded me in practical daily matters so that I couldn't go "out there." It was as though I would like to "go crazy" with what had just happened to me, but I'd only have time from 5:00 PM to 5:15 PM because all of my time would be spent getting three children ready for school, car pooling, driving to after-school swim team, cooking, cleaning, doing laundry (mountains and mountains of laundry!), operating a fine-art gallery, meditating, and acclimating to my NDE.

The NDE and I were like new best friends. It was an experience that I took with me everywhere. I nicknamed the NDE, "Ned." Yes, Ned had become my new best friend and has been with me ever since, just standing over my shoulder gently telling me, "Go For It." You can do it!" When I would have self doubt about telling my story to people, or when the "stinking thinking" of "who do I think I am?" would set in, I would feel Ned's tall strength looking over my shoulder, quietly saying, "Just speak your truth about your experience: not anyone else's, just yours. That is all you have to do." Easy for you to say, Ned! I would think and find a hundred thousand other things to do rather than talk about my NDE.

It seemed as though something magical would happen if I could muster the nerve and share my NDE story with someone, usually a complete stranger or friend of a friend whom I'd just met at a social gathering. I would be given a "go ahead" sign, like a voice in my head that I couldn't turn off, or an uncomfortable, overwhelming feeling in the pit of my stomach, that said that this person needed to hear my story. After sharing, the listener would invariably tell me his or her own extraordinary experience about an extraterrestrial visitor in their room at night; a loved one who had passed over appearing at the foot of their bed; a pet that had died, swooshing across the back of their legs while they were doing dishes; a spirit guide with whom they'd had an ongoing relationship since childhood; an NDE of their own; or a loved one's story. The list of extraordinary experiences went on and on.

Guidance

A genuine sense that the Earth was being monitored by such a loving group of ecstatic beings, like the Watchers, calmed me down. I could perhaps rely on something bigger than myself, who had everything in order. I don't mean that we came to just sit here and do nothing; if anything, I mean the complete opposite. We are given an opportunity in this lifetime to change the things that we see are not in order. Not only creating a presence of healing individually, but collectively, as humans existing on Planet Earth at this time.

Maybe it is not a new story, but I am fired up and ready for action. I am capable of letting go of the past and dreaming a new dream, a positive life filled with love, passion and beauty. Not only a new, more vibrant life for myself, but for all of humanity.

My dream would be that my grandchildren would not know what the concept of the word "war" meant. Because war had become so archaic in their lifetimes, my great-grandchildren would shake their heads with disbelief. The fact that in the past we allowed something so violent and ongoing to occur simply could not exist in their reality.

I understand that we must fight for our freedom. I salute the soldiers everywhere, and every time a soldier dies for whatever reason, I feel his or her family's pain, because it is our pain. What we choose individually affects the whole of society. I guess I am saying that if we can dream peace as a collective then it can become a reality of peace on this planet now. How about if there was going to be a war, but no one showed up? Everyone took a stand and said, "No." No more war. We have to find a better way to resolve our differences.

The dream for humanity that was given to me by the Watchers was that we are not alone in the Cosmos, and that we are being watched with love, honor, and respect. One of these days, hopefully in the near future, we can grow up and play nice with the rest of the Universe before it is too late. Until then, we can be a peaceful and loving humanity, and we have that choice to say no to violence and war. I am not saying that we should be a doormat, and let greed; power and control have their way with a gentle, peace-loving race of humans, but that we must find other solutions. And we will, if war and violence were just not an option.

Love & Compassion

Since my NDE, I have had many hills and valleys of life's lessons. The fact is that we are never alone. We are surrounded by many loving and caring teachers, spirit-guides, and loved ones who will help shine light in the darkness.

The choice is yours of how you want to spend the precious time that you are given. If you want to take time to know yourself and what you truly value in life, not only for yourself but for future generations, it will take courage, strength, and endurance – but also it can be achieved. Like a lump of coal turning into a bright, shining diamond, it takes the alchemy of time, and focused intention and energy, to transform.

We have the power of love instilled within us that will never die. This spark of the Divine is your birthright, and it is so powerful. Hold on and reach down within, and build a relationship with it that is so strong that you can trust it and let it guide you through life's journey of experiences, changes, growth, transformation, and enlightenment.

At first it probably will be outside your comfort zone – like losing your job or having your longtime relationship suddenly end – and you are cast out into a new world, alone and frightened. Just reach out, let go, and remember that we come from love, we are love, we return to love, and we never die. Love is available always, like nature changing her seasons naturally, and that fact is something you can depend on.

Peace

After many years since my NDE, I have come to realize the fact that peace and joy through love is a lifestyle of which I am a devotee. My hope is that I have inspired you to get to know who you are and why you are here. My wish for you is that you take that information, and have a glorious life for yourself and your loved ones while transforming our planet.

The experience of death set me free to really live a more fearless life, as I was assured through unconditional love that we as humans are so amazingly loved and loving. We have a creative spark connected within us that is begging to be expressed artistically in some way, if we would take the time to discover it. This connection, when we find the zone, can offer such a sense of reward and fulfillment.

I found out that for me, connecting with spirit meant searching out the esoteric healing arts. Music and dancing with people on the dance floor shaking off any worries, problems, or negative thoughts would sometimes be the perfect medicine. Reminding me that if I took a moment in each day and gave thanks and connected to "Great Spirit," or a higher power, that I could relax and develop a greater sense of knowing. If I did the practical applications of life (namely work), then saved part of myself for expression of the Divine, then a door would open that would help guide and nurture me into doing something more amazingly incredible with my life than I could even imagine for myself.

I am committed to being vital. I was more alive during my death than I ever had been when alive. Since the near death experience, my new best friend, Ned, would ride on my shoulder, gently pushing me to take more chances, get uncomfortable. Ned said to change things up… and so I did.

Instead of focusing on keeping my head low, working hard, being "thankful, grateful," blending with society's accepted normal, I set off on a wild adventure to find out who I am and why I am here. To live each day as best I could, while not letting go of the truth that I came from the Stars.

There was another odd thing that seemed to happen since I had my near death experience. I had several people who commented that they just felt better being around me.

Peace is deep in me now and I feel like I don't sweat the small things anymore. It feels like that when I am around people now: I tend to talk to them "spirit to spirit," that is, directly to the heart.

A Pleasure to Serve

This has been my NDE story. It has taken me over twenty-five years to write it. Sometimes I think it has taken me so long to write because I was still trying to put all the pieces together in a complete, perfect picture before I presented it to you. The truth is that life is a never-ending process, and it is definitely not going to be perfect, ever. What is the fun in that?

By giving more than taking in this world, and by leaving it a better place than when we found it, the next generations will have a chance to enjoy this amazing planet, Mother Earth. A teacher of mine told me that if you want to find out who you are in this world, the best way is to do it is through service work for humanity. By working alongside others, helping people, and making a difference for the positive in their lives, you will discover who you truly are and why you are here. Do I hear any volunteers?

With a little help from my friends, family, and mentors along the way, I am planning on celebrating life's adventure by loving more, dancing as often as I can, listening to music, writing, being aware of things that I can change for the better for humanity, and taking right action.

Bringing It All Home

I had different ideas of what my accepted mission as an "Ambassador" meant. An authorized representative or messenger are examples of the definitions of "Ambassador" in the dictionary. That sounds about right! I am an Ambassador. But what kind of Ambassador was I?

Since I owned an art gallery, maybe I was an Ambassador for the arts. Then, I thought that maybe I was an Ambassador between the worlds. Then I thought that maybe I was an Ambassador of the Cosmos. Then I thought maybe I was an Ambassador of love. Then I thought maybe I was an Ambassador for Women's Spiritual Healing & Empowerment. Then I thought maybe I was an Ambassador for Humanity and Extra-terrestrials. Then I thought maybe I was an Ambassador for Inter-Dimensional Realities and Perspectives. Then I realized I was an Ambassador in Progress and the future will determine my destiny.

We have always been free to have a choice in how we want to live this life. Don't let anyone take that from you ever, not even the illusion of death. The truth is that we are immortal. We come from love, we are love, and we return to love. We never die.

I will continue to embrace the mysteries and gifts the universe has to offer, for there are so many. I know that we never walk alone, and that flame of love within us will continue to light the way in the darkness.

After this life, we continue through into the After-life, bright shining like the sun, the moon, and the stars of the Cosmos with which we are connected. We return naturally, once again, to that familiar White Light of love from which we first originated.

It has been a pleasure to serve.
Barbara Jean Lindsey
Ambassador

The End

Acknowledgments

I began thinking of writing this book over twenty-five years ago after my NDE first happened. It has been a wild ride and without the help and support of so many people on this journey, this book would not be here today. I am so thankful and grateful to so many...

This book is dedicated to my three amazing children, Ryan, Melody and Audrey as we have been together through all the changes, growth and transformation from the very beginning. They have always supported me with such genuine love, caring and wisdom beyond their age. I love you all so much.

Ryan, thank you for being selflessly dedicated to the completion of this book. It could not have been written without you.

A special thank you to my Sister, Terri, for her unwavering foundation of love and positive feedback, as I needed it along the way. A special thank you to my mother, Elsie, for her generosity and belief in me. Special thanks to my Daughter-In-Law, Mika McDonald, Son-in-Law, Zack Kent, and Danny Diaz for all of your love and continued support you bring to the family. To my brother Kenny Lindsey and Tambi, my Sister, Donna Schroeder.

Thank you to my three Grandchildren, Elliot Michael, Octavia Scarlett and Briton James for bringing such joy and blessings to my heart and soul. Your laughter lifts me up and inspires me.

Special thank you to Dannion and Kathryn Brinkley for your time, inspiration and generosity. I am so grateful.

A heartfelt thank you to my amazing editor and friend, Ronnie Rennae, for having the patience and heart of an Angel and her ability to intuit the true vision of the birthing of this book.

This book would not have been possible without Tom Bird Writing Seminars and Publishing with a special thank you to Rama Jon and all that you do for so many.

There are special people, teachers, coaches and friends that showed up in my life at just the right time and helped propel this book along for which I am forever grateful: Hariharananda Giri, Normandi Ellis, Nikki Scully, Gloria Taylor-Brown, Robert Perala, Gwen Thomas, Mike Swift, Alyson Vanderbeck, Jan Newell, Marna Van Horn, Johanna Bautzer, Nickie Nicholas, Cyndee Schaefer, Frank Moncrief, Paula Turtletaub, Ellias Lonsdale, Aurelia Scherf, Barbara Lamb, Richard Boylan, Dempsey Harshaw, Dave Alan, Hollandia Mass, Erin McCauliff, Kathy Jones, Iris Finsilver, Laura Janesdaughter, Michael Koplen, Robert Haberkorn, Tim Walter, Raven Grimassi and Emily Green

About the Author

Barbara Jean Lindsey is an internationally-acclaimed psychic, spiritual teacher and inspirational speaker.

In 1989, Barbara Jean had an extraordinary Near-Death-Experience; after full-body channeling an ancient Egyptian being, her lungs collapsed, almost killing her in front of a live audience. Over the next two days she fought for her life (on the physical plane, spiritual plane and beyond). Barbara Jean's story, journey and transformation are chronicled in her autobiography, "Dying For the Light."

Following her NDE, Barbara Jean has appeared on and hosted numerous television, radio, online and live event programs, including the "Cosmic Cafe Experiencer's Meetup" at the annual Contact in the Desert Conference and the weekly, "Cosmic Oracle Show," on the Revolution Radio Network. www.freedomslips.com

She is the Dean and Founder of Esoteric University, an online mystery school for metaphysical studies. (www.EsotericUniversity.com) www.Facebook/Esoteric University

As Executive Director of the nonprofit 501C3, "Casa Del Sol," Barbara Jean sponsors and facilitates the annual "Heart of the Cosmic Woman" Conference, a gathering of women that empowers, inspires and heals women through celebrating the Goddess.

She has continued her private psychic counseling practice for over twenty-five years.

Barbara Jean currently lives with her son, daughter-in-law and grandson in Lyon, France where she pursues her passions in the arts, history and antique collecting.

She still loves nachos.

www.BarbaraJeanLindsey.com

A New Beginning

This book is written for a wide variety of people. In telling my story so many times over the years, I really found that I had gained a shorthand of a lot of terms that "average" people, myself included before my NDE, wouldn't have known the meanings of half of them. Below you will find a Glossary with my loose interpretation of commonly used terms throughout the book. I hope you find it helpful.

Just like in the Chapter, *Wrapping my Brain Around It*, now that you have finished reading the book, you might be asking yourself, "What is *my* next step?" I can't tell you that, first of all, because I am just pages in a book. Secondly, because ultimately, it is your life and it is different from everybody else.

We each have a unique life experience with the freedom to make choices along the way which will ultimately affect our quality of life. I chose not to live a life of regrets, become bitter, walk away from responsibility or blame it all on something or somebody else. I challenged myself to delve into the mysteries of life and challenge the conditioning of what I had been told was the truth, how to act and what to do.

Change takes courage and commitment and it can be terrifying in the beginning, a bit like a fool jumping over a cliff, a train going off the track, or jumping into the deep end of a pool when you can't swim. It gets easier with time, as I began to trust myself and my instincts, I found that there were always helpers, teachers and spirit guides directing me along the way, if I took time to tune in and listen.

After the Glossary, stick around because I've gathered a "Best of" with links to websites, forums and other resources for those who may be interested in learning a little more about the topics in this book. If you prefer your information in long-form, there is a nice collection of books for more in-depth information. Finally, if you are interested in taking the jump yourself, I've listed online groups, conferences and in-person places to meet other like-minded people in a safe environment.

I thought I would write a simple book about my NDE/contact and that would be it. The apex of my life had been my death, so the re-telling of that event should be the end-all, be-all with nothing following. In the years of researching, writing and writing *Dying for the Light,* I found that my death had not been the end, but a new beginning. It served as a catalyst, propelling me further in my search for truth and self realization.

My story continues in *Ambassador for the Light*. As a fellow seeker of truth, I invite you to come with me as I recount my travels to sacred spots and with spiritual people around the world: drumming with Chief Geronimo III in Arizona, 23 psychic surgeries in the Philippines, meditating in Merlin's cave in England, chilling in an Airstream trailer with Billy Meier in Switzerland, writing at the base between the Sphinx's paws in Egypt, chasing UFOs at the historic Integratron (which I co-owned at the time), visiting St. Bernadette's Grotto in Lourdes, France, teaching a fire walking seminar in Joshua Tree, spending three god-intoxicated days of bliss with Hariharananda Giri at his ashram in Florida and many more...

A journey of twenty-five years continues in my true story, *Ambassador for the Light.* Let's continue this journey together...

Glossary

Afterlife: Where we transition to after we have fully disconnected from our body, but as spirit still exist. We can be greeted by our loved ones and/or pets who have transitioned as well. We are never alone in this process.

Alien: A being from a variety of backgrounds, shapes, colors and sizes from another world or dimension that can look and feel very different from us and they usually prefer to communicate telepathically.

Alien Abduction: A person is taken against his or her will from their home, or car or natural environment by non-human beings and transported usually onto an alien space craft and can be subjected to an examination and or communicated to by telepathic language.

Alternate Reality: A time in space that exists even though we can't see it unless we are in an altered state of consciousness.

Aura: An active and invisible (can be seen clairvoyantly) energetic field, like an electrical field, emanating from and surrounding all living things.

Aura Healing: Balancing one's unseen auric field that surrounds the natural body by removing blockages to the aura by gently moving one's hands along the outside of the aura and filling in with White Light.

Ambassador: Is an honest and heart felt representative for his or her country or planet who travels to a foreign country, planet, time or space.

Angel: A spiritual being who is believed to be a messenger of God or Goddess who doesn't necessarily have to be male, female or have wings, a sword or a perfectly sculpted body, but usually have a beautiful out of this world presence.

Awareness: To be in the state of the loving mindfulness of all existence as you go about the business of daily living one thought and one step at a time.

Bliss: A peak spiritual experience that reminds you that you come from something amazingly wonderful beyond yourself.

Celestial: The boundless love and intelligence of the heavens. I think I hear joyous singing!

Channeling: When someone begins to sound not like their natural self because another entity/personality has entered the body and has temporarily claimed use of the vocal chords to speak out loud information being received psychically; usually done safely after much training and awareness.

Coma: The body is in a deep sleep but the spirit and owner of the body isn't home.

Consciousness: The everyday state of being in which you are awake and aware of yourself and your surroundings in relationship with yourself, the Earth and the Cosmos.

Cosmic Pulse: The beat (like a drum) of the cosmos.

Cosmos: A harmonious and complete order of the Divine that we haven't been able to see the end of, yet.

Death: We have successfully disconnected from the body and are moving on our way into the afterlife.

Divine Spark: A piece of the big fire of the divine light of all life everywhere, that dwells within each and everyone of us.

Earth Mother: Our planet is ancient and of the wise feminine.

Empathy: To feel what another person's feeling. As if you were in their body and could suddenly walk around in it and feel everything they are feeling.

Energy: It is what makes us move and have the desire to remember, move and create.

Enlightenment: Finding deep peace and connection within the natural laws of the universe – Big Happy Face, rainbows, unicorns and sunshine, hahahahaha.

Esoteric: Secret and hidden knowledge from ancient mystery schools.

Etheric: Energy that you can't see but you know it is there.

Fear: An awareness of something or someone that you are extremely afraid of and then you have to overcome the challenge it represents to heal yourself and/or others.

God: The man upstairs and within lovingly guiding you with your best interest at heart always and with hopefully, a sense of humor.

Goddess: The woman upstairs and within lovingly guiding you with your best interest at heart always and with hopefully, a sense of humor.

Hallucination: A thought or thoughts that are an illusion(s) but you buy what it is selling you as being really real.

Halo: A radiant and glowing white light surrounding the head of a highly evolved person, also known as, "fire in the head," as seen in ancient texts and paintings.

Healer: A sensitive person who knows the needs of others and who has developed their innate skills to alleviate pain and suffering and instill change for the better.

Healing: Changing negative and diseased energy into a positive healing force.

Higher Power: A positive force that is bigger than you can even imagine.

"High Strangeness": When things start to go a little bit off and you can't put it into words, but it feels really weird and not normal at all. Usually can be present when people are in contact with UFO's or aliens.

Holograph: The big picture of the whole of something in light form.

Holy Spirit: The light force of God in White Light form.

Hospice: Loving and respectful supportive care for a person transitioning to the Afterlife.

Infinite Awareness: Beyond the mind which cannot be measured but imagined.

Inter-Dimensional: A different channel than the one you are currently residing within and acting upon.

Intergalactic Being: Space brother and/or sister.

Intuition: Tapping into a gut feeling and instinctively knowing that something is true without the need for conscious reasoning.

Light: Overcomes the darkness as a powerful force to be reckoned with.

Love: Is Divine source of what we are made of and what keeps us together. (Sounds much like a song from the singing Duo, Captain and Tennille in 1975)

Life: The experience of being vital and the ability to grow, change and evolve.

Meditation: An epic technique to achieve a higher state of consciousness.

Metaphysician: One who develops and works with the knowledge of the spiritual nature of being, changing and growing.

Midwife: A person of knowledge and birthing skills, who aids the mother, child and family during the phases of childbirth and delivery.

Miracle: A wondrous event of Divine intervention, effect beyond human capabilities.

Moon (Earth's): An object that moves around Earth which affects the tides of the ocean, crop plantings, women's cycles and gets its' light reflected from the Sun. My daughter's bath and body boutique – www.MoonSoaps.com

Multiverse: Comprises many universes including our own as one

Near death experience: When a person comes very close to dying or declared clinically dead but finds their spirit or life force still exists outside their physical body and then brings back memories of that spiritual experience to share with others.

Omnipotent: All Powerful Big Kahuna of Everything of All That Was, Is and Will Be! Thunder clouds loudly rolling and lightening bolts clashing in the sky ceremoniously over your head, as you read this.

Open Mind: Willing to consider ideas or opinions even if they are different than your own and might make you feel uncomfortable at first.

Possession: To enter into a person's mind and body and take over where the spirit once resided without permission and with evil intent.

Prayer: Powerful act of asking for help from God/Goddess/Deity of your choice with expectation that you will be heard and your request answered.

Psychic: The ability in an altered state of consciousness to sense or know information that you normally can't access through the five senses.

Psychic Reading: Neutrally sense, understand and interpret subtle vibrations, energies and information from the beyond and then give practical ways to work with the information received.

Psychic School: Helps educate, train and promote psychic awareness and abilities.

Quest: A hero or heroine's journey for knowledge.

Quiet: A meditative state of being centered, relaxed and free.

Soul: The breath that gives of life in life.

Spiral: A coil of etheric energy of change, growth and evolution.

Spirit Guide: A mighty guardian or protector that you can build a relationship with even though most people can't actually see them without psychic training.

Spirit-to-spirit: Information exchanged from one being to another beyond personal consciousness, time and space usually from the heart to the heart.

Spiritual: Openness to the Divine nature's intangible energy and movement of love.

Talking in Tongues: A mild hypnotic state of ecstasy where your teeth can chatter and you talk in a foreign or unknown language, rapidly bringing pleasure and connection with the Holy Spirit through the entire body.

Telepathic: Ability to send and receive messages directly through thought forms quickly without a sound.

Temple: A building or an area in nature that serves as a meeting place to conduct ongoing services, education or performance of ceremonies and/or rituals.

Unconsciousness: Being uniformed and unaware and missing out on something really amazing going on all around you.

Universal Law: A golden rule that is upheld based on all that we think we know.

Vibrations: Feelings of a person's emotional state communicated to and felt by others without speaking words.

Near Death Experience Resources

Online Links:

IANDS: International Association For Near Death Studies
Website: http://iands.org

This is the "Grand Daddy" of all of the Near Death Experience websites, the one that I believe has made the biggest impact and over the longest period of time encouraging independent research and education on a global scale. On their site it states the following: **IANDS has helped change the public perception of what it is like to die.** This statement is so true.

NHNE Near-Death Experience Network
http://nhneneardeath.ning.com

This is a colorful and happy website exploring all the aspects of near-death experiences and related subjects. Expect to spend some time on this site. I did.

The Nour Foundation
Exploring Meaning and & Commonality in Human Experience
Website: http://www.nourfoundation.com

This foundation was Inspired by the philosophy of Ostad Elahi, who spent the majority of his life exploring the age old questions, "Who are we? Where did we come from? Why are we here?"

I found this site to be a stimulating and thought provoking website. It is based in New York, so need I say more? Give it a look.

Institute of Noetic Sciences
Website: http://noetic.org

The Institute of Noetic Sciences was founded by the late great Edgar Mitchel. After becoming the 6ᵗʰ man to walk on the moon and coming back to earth, his life was changed forever and so the Institute of Noetic Sciences began its' distinguished long time service in the exploration of consciousness and human potential.

I found this website to be easy and a user friendly atmosphere with access to articles relating to research, education and how you can become engaged with communities worldwide. Awesome website with lots of solid information, videos, classes and event listings, etc. My favorite article was the research being done on the phenomena of consciousness transformation. How can it occur? How can it be stimulated?

Near Death Experience Foundation
Website: http://www.nderf.org

A quote on their website that I just love:

"If enough people read about love, peace and hope: maybe they can change to become more loving, compassionate people who truly live their lives without fear. We can change the world to become a better place like heaven on earth – as above, so below."

The Institute for Afterlife Research (IAR) & The Institute for Afterlife Studies(IAS)
Website: http://www.mikepettigrew.com/afterlife

This website is based in Ireland and they know some friends of mine, I gave it a look and loved it. It is a bit dated but the information regarding death and dying and the Afterlife is still well written and you can gather a lot of information quickly and easily. When I go to Ireland in the fall of 2016, I plan on meeting the founders, Mike and Helen Feiffer and having a chat about their extraordinary experiences which proved to them beyond any doubt, the existence of the Afterlife. Afterwards, I will let you know how it turned out.

NHNE Near-Death Experience Network
http://nhneneardeath.ning.com

Exploring all aspects of near-death experiences (and related phenomena).

A beautiful website inventive with a focus on NDE stories. NHNE Near-Death Experience Network is a non-profit organization based in Sedona, Arizona and offers, like they say, a tsunami of information about the NDE. They have a Facebook page and a video channel on YouTube. I especially liked the video posted, "What Near Death Experiences Teach Us." I posted the links below for you to explore, like I did. I became a member as well.

https://www.facebook.com/nhnende
https://www.youtube.com/user/nhnemultimedia

Near-Death Experts

Listed below are just a few of the near-death experts that I admire. Through their scientific research at the time, these "Way Showers," helped me realize that NDE's were absolutely not happening from malfunctioning brains! That everyone could grow from the knowledge brought back from the NDE to reflect and inspire one's own life and others. The late Dr. John Mack was a visionary in this field of research.

PMH Atwater:	www.pmhatwater.com
Victor Egger:	Originally coined the phrase, "NDE" in 1895.
Elisabeth Kubler-Ross:	www.EKRFoundation.org
Dr. John Mack:	www.johnemackinstitute.org
Raymond Moody:	www.lifeafterlife.com
Kenneth Ring:	www.kenring.org
Charles Tart:	www.paradigm-sys.com

Near-Death Experience Movies

A really huge website for current classes, movies and spiritual information:

Website: www.Gaia.com

The List below offers many videos for rent or purchase under the title, "Near Death Experience."

Website: www.Amazon.com
Website: www.Netflix.com

Near-Death Experience stories

I loved this website with videos of the NDE'ers telling their stories in person.
www.plus.google.com/collection/08kix

Books:

Where do I begin with my love for books? Let me count the ways…

I was on a mission to figure out what had happened to me. Books were my first choice to help find some answers. In 1989, we had no internet or cell phones, so books were the premium source of information. I had not heard of the term, NDE and any contact with aliens had been the farthest thing from my mind before my NDE and contact.

So, I quickly amassed a huge library of books on a variety of subjects of the NDE, including history, art, religion, psychic awareness, philosophy, alternative healing, scientific research, human potential, consciousness, death and dying, etc. In 1989, we had no internet or cell phones, so, books were the premium source of how to gather information. Below I have listed, what I think are some of the best books as a beginning on the subject of the NDE.

Saved by the Light by **Dannion Brinkley** – A true story about how he died twice and the revelations he received, An absolute classic!

Embraced by the Light by **Betty J. Eadie** – A small book that packs a huge wallop and top of the list of best NDE books to me.

Dying to be Me by **Anita Moorjani** – A truly inspirational book about dying, healing cancer and unconditional love.

Proof of Heaven by **Eben Alexander** – A neuro surgeon's NDE that questions his previous knowledge of the science of dying and death.

Life After Life by **Raymond Moody & Elizabeth Kubler Ross** – The "Dynamic Duo," with over 13 million copies sold. Need I say more?

Divine Blueprint by **Robert Perala and Tony Stubbs** – An "out of this world" true story, of one man's abduction and his spiritual journey, with many shared insights and words of wisdom.

Evidence of the Afterlife by **Jeffrey Long with Paul Perry** – It is all about the science of NDE's created with such dedication for the truth.

Beyond the Light by **P.M.H. Atwater** – Being and experiencer, she writes with such insightful clarity, a true visionary.

The Place We Call Home by **Robert J. Grant** – One of my favorites, I brought it to France with me and love the references to Edgar Cayce.

***Beyond Death*, Visions of the Other Side** by **Edgar Cayce** – A true visionary, psychic and healer. There was my "Edgar Cayce" period when I had to try and read everything this brilliant man had ever written.

The Handbook of Near Death Experiences by **Janice Miner Holden & Bruce Greyson** – The handbook of handbooks of NDE scientific research.

Life at Death by **Dr. Kenneth Ring** confirms Dr. Moody's research on NDE with his ground breaking experience and research.

***Awakening Osiris*, The Egyptian Book of the Dead** by **Normandi Ellis** – A must read of this poetic and powerful translation of the soul's journey. I had the privilege of being a student of writing, with the brilliant, Normandi Ellis, as we cruised down the Nile from Aswan in upper Egypt toward Luxor on the dahabia, "Afandina."

My Life After Dying by **George G. Ritchie, Jr., MD** – A truly heroic story about his journey into the mysteries of life.

Forums:

There are many forums to be found but these are two of my favorites.

http://nhneneardeath.ning.com
http://nhneneardeath.ning.com/forum

Experiencer's Groups - Online

Website: www.groups.yahoo.com/neo/groups/NDE-support-group/info
Group Description:

A "support group" for people who've had a near-death experience (NDE). The post-NDE period can be one of isolation, confusion and wonderment. Here, NDE'ers can discuss the event itself, assimilate resulting thoughts & feelings, and deal with any repercussions following this often life-changing event.

Website: **www.meetup.com/topics/neardeathexp**
Group Description:

Meet others who've had a near-death experience (NDE), out-of-body experience (OBE), or spiritually transformative experience (STE). Gather to freely and openly have candid discussions about your experiences, concerns and needs, without fear, in a space that's very supportive. It is a loving environment where all can share in the profundity of these life-altering events that change and transform our lives forever. Individuals interested in NDEs are also welcome.

Website: www.iands.org/groups/affiliated-groups/ find-a-group.html

Group Description:

IANDS groups can be found in communities around the world, meeting to talk about and share near-death experiences, questions about death and dying, and the latest information from NDE research.

If you can't find a website, forum or meet up that works for you, you can always start your own with a little help from your friends …

Just a Few Near Death Experience Conferences:

A.R.E. Virginia Beach Conferences - www.edgar cayce.org

Dying and Death Conference - www.Inter-disciplinary.net

Esalen Center Conferences - www.esalenctr.org

Intl. Association for Near-Death Studies Conference - www.iands.org

The Afterlife Awareness Conference - www.afterlife conference.com

UFO & Contact Resources

Online Links:
Paradigm Research Group
Website: www.paradigmresearchgroup.org

Steven Bassett is the executive director and was the founder of PRG in 1996. Since then he has spoken to audiences around the world and over 1000 radio shows and the list goes on and on of his relentless and passionate drive to have the real truth behind the "UFO" phenomenon disclosed to the people. He produced a "Citizen Hearing on Disclosure at the National Press Club in Washington DC in 2014 and launched a Congressional Hearing/Political Initiative.

July 8th World Disclosure Day
Website: www.paradigmresearchgroup.org/WDD_ Contribute.htm

The primary mission for World Disclosure day is to provide a platform for people and organizations of all nations to stand together in support of the world's right to know the truth regarding an extraterrestrial presence engaging the human race. With your help there is no limit of what can be accomplished including one million endorsements, special events and broad media coverage.

Center for the Study of Extraterrestrial Intelligence
CSETI
Website: www. new.cseti.org

Was founded in 1990 by Dr. Steven M Greer. This worldwide organization is dedicated to open public education regarding extra terrestrial intelligence and they are diligently working on the ongoing Disclosure Project.

They lead ongoing Ambassador Training expeditions. I attended one of Dr. Greer's trainings, way back in the day in Joshua Tree near Giant Rock. While searching in the dark skies at night, if you want to communicate with others where you are locating a space ship, you can imagine the sky as a clock, so you can easily communicate with others, where you see that space ship by shouting out, "I have lock on at 9:00PM or 6:00PM like the hands on a large sky clock, whatever time you see. I really enjoyed the training and I met some really cool people.
www.siriusdisclosure.com

Mutual UFO Network
MUFON
Website:WWW.mufon.com

One of the oldest organizations dedicated to the UFO phenomena. You can train with MUFON and become part of their investigative team. How cool is that? Their website has current sighting reports, a newsroom, research updates and more.

Barbara Jean Lindsey

UFO and Paranormal Research Society
UPARS
Website: www.meetup.com/UPARS-Los-Angeles

Founded by Steve Murillo in Los Angeles. UPARS investigates all things UFO and paranormal. I attended many monthly meetings which have a featured speaker with a question and answer session at the end. I met some very interesting people there. In fact, I met the person who said I should be on her friend, Ivy West's radio show in Hawaii. While I was on Ivy's show, the founder of Revolution Radio, www.freedomslips.com, happened to be listening and asked me if I wanted my own show. I said, "Yes!" That is how the weekly Cosmic Oracle Radio Show began and it continues today. I give free psychic readings for people as one of my gifts of service back to community.
www.facebook.com/events/1377648262505617/

Mutual UFO Network-France
Mufon-France
Website: http://www.les-rencontres-ufologiques.com

Since I have been living in Lyon, France, I have been visiting this website. I have yet to attend a meeting but really looking forward to attending one soon. Although, Jacques Patenet, the National Director, has stepped down from his post, due to his disenchantment given of the evolution of ufology. Yikes!

Australian Close Encounter Research Network
ACERN
Website: www.acern.com.au
Website: www.Facebook.com/acern.com.au

Founded in 1996 by Mary Rodwell. ACERN is a professional resource and support network for close encounter experiencers and research. The first time I heard her speak, I said to myself, "Who is that person? I must meet her." She is a brilliant presenter and writer.

The Dr. Edgar Mitchell Foundation for Research into Extraterrestrial Encounters
Website: www.experiencer.org

A Not for Profit Research Organization founded on July 15, 2015. This is one of the best organizations and you can really feel the hearts of all those who are a part of this team. To me, it feels genuinely true where science and consciousness research can meet to create change for the positive regarding UFO contact and paranormal investigations and much more. Out of five stars being the highest, I would give this organization and website five stars. You have to check it out! So much to continue to learn…

Ufologists

I must admit that these articles do a fantastic job much better than I have the patience for, so enjoy! …

The 100 Most Influential People in Ufology Today by Fate Magazine – 2005 Special

Barbara Jean Lindsey

http://human-science-research.blogspot.fr/2005/06
/100-most-influential-people-in-ufology.html
http://ufodigest.com/article/world%E2%80%99s-top-
ufologists

Contact Experience Stories:
http://freedom-articles.toolsforfreedom.com/top-20-
alien-contactee-abductee-part-1/

TRAVIS The True Story of Travis Walton – One
man's survival after a terrifying journey

Some Books that Helped Me Along the Way...

Serpent in the Sky by John Anthony West – Was the
first book that I read after my NDE/contact. I needed to
know everything I could about Egypt and had developed an insatiable passion for ancient history. Love this
book and this man! I have been to Egypt twice but really want to go at least once more and hopefully with
John Anthony West, as the tour guide.

Chariot's of the Gods by **Ercih Von Danniken** – The
grandfather of the ancient astronaut theorist movement.
This book changed my life.

The Sacred Pipe by **Michael F. Steltenkamp** – Black
Elk, Holy Man of the Oglala's account of the seven
rites of the Oglala Sioux was an important book for me
when I was searching for a spiritual relationship with
the Earth.

104

The Encyclopedic Psychic Dictionary by **June G. Bletzer, Ph.D.** – The best psychic reference book, like no other, hands down.

Got Ghosts??? by **Ronnie Rennae Foster & Laura Lee Mistycah** – An insightful book of knowledge, wisdom and practical advice with a few goose bumps, wit and humor.

Left at East Gate by **Larry Warren & Peter Robbins** – An important, gripping and compelling first-hand account of a true UFO experience, investigation and cover-up and its' life long aftereffects.

Awakening by **Mary Rodwell** – a trained counselor's point of view written with compassion and tremendous insights for the novice and the trained professional regarding the UFO abduction phenomenon. Well done!

Fingerprints of the Gods & Magicians of the Gods both books by *Graham* Hancock – Two thought provoking masterpieces that are a "must have," if you are building a library and research into ancient civilizations and consciousness.

Communion by **Whitley Strieber** – One of the first books that I read about a true story of contact which the book cover alone scared the crap out of me, but it is listed here, none the less.

Captured! **The Betty & Barney Hill UFO Experience** by **Stanton T. Friedman & Kathleen Marden** – An historic couple's recollection of alien abduction and their separate hypnotherapy sessions. This true story is written by Betty's niece and Stanton Freidman, a physicist and Ufologist with a renown world-class reputation; a knockout combination.

Fire in the Sky by **Travis Walton & Mike Rogers** – One of the best documented cases of alien abduction and was also made into a popular movie. I met Travis Walton and talked with him briefly. He was really friendly and seemed like an honest and easy going kind of fella.

Close Extraterrestrial Encounter by **Dr. Richard J. Boylan & Lee K. Boylan** – A book dedicated to positive close encounter stories. I met Dr. Boylan at the *Evolving Times Expo* in Sacramento where I taught a pubic fire walking seminar. We became friends as Dr. Boylan and his wife, Lee, held "Experiencer" monthly meetings in their homes. These meetings were so invaluable to me at the beginning of my journey of acclimation back into society after my NDE and contact.

Alien Agenda by **Jim Marrs** – An award winning journalist and author and one of the best books on UFO's. Mr. Marrs investigates the UFO and abduction cases, theories, cover-ups and more while giving accurate information.

Technology of the Gods: The Incredible Sciences of the Ancient by **David Hatcher Childress** – A thought provoking and stimulating book of ideas, theories, hard facts and ancient theory. Loved it!

The Andreasson Affair by **Raymond E. Fowler & Dr. J. Allen Hynek** – First published in 1979 and re-published again in 2015, this book is about the true abduction story of Betty Andreasson. It will rock your world!

UFO's for the 21ˢᵗ Century Mind by **Richard Doylan** – One of my more recent favorites. Deliciously well written with invaluable information and historic accuracy.

Flying Saucers Have Landed by ***George* Adamski** – Nothing like reading an "old school" classic written by an historic figure in the field of Ufology. Finding some of my most favorite books in garage sales, flea markets and used book stores, is much like treasure hunting, you never know what jewel of a book, you may discover.

Forums:
https://www.facebook.com/groups/FREE.Experiencers/
https://www.alien-ufos.com

One of the most active alien and UFO websites on the internet. That is what they say!

Contact Groups Online:
East Bay UFO/ET Contact Group
Website: http://www.meetup.com/East-Bay-UFO-ET-Contact-Group/
Contactees, Experiencers and Starseeds who wish to share their experiences…

UFOContact.com
A UFO contact community of 5,000 like minded members in 50+ countries gathering together.
They offer simple directions to follow on, " Creating a Contact Experience with ET Intelligence."
They have a UFO/ET community map.

Australia UFO Action
A.U.F.O.A
Website: https://www.facebook.com/AUFOA
Australia's premier UFO investigation and research. Founded in 2007.They have teams of investigators who cover the entire states of Australia.

Contact Conferences:
After attending the "Cosmic Culture Conference" in 1995, I attended conventions regularly for years. Meeting inquisitive, like-minded people from such diverse backgrounds while learning so much, that I thought my mind might melt. It was the perfect ticket that I needed to explore this new world, beyond the five senses, that had opened up for me. What is really cool nowadays is that many of the conventions offer live "mainstreaming" of the events. So, even if you can't attend, you can

get the information, while relaxing in the comfort of your own home.

Contact in the Desert
CITD
Website: contactinthedesert.com

An epic weekend of exploration into ancient astronauts, extraterrestrial life, human origins, ancient aliens, crop circles, UFO sightings, contact experiences and the "need to know." Featuring a thrilling lineup of the best of the best extraordinary speakers with lectures, workshops and UFO night watching. Erich Von Danniken, Giorgio A. Tsoukalos, David Wilcock, Alan Feinstein, Laura Eisenhower, James Gilliland and George Norry just to name a few of the world renown speakers and presenters.

I host the Cosmic Café Experiencer's Lounge during the conference. We create a collaborative sharing space for everyone who has experienced something beyond themselves; from the Extra-Terrestrial (UFOs and ETs) to the spiritual (OBEs and Altered States.) Through open discussion, camaraderie and acceptance, we dispel fear and isolation and open the door for all people to share their stories. Maybe I will see you there? Don't forget to stop by and say, "hello."

M.U.F.O.N. Symposium
Website:
https://www.facebook.com/mufonsymposium
During the international symposium, you can explore the mystery of the UFO enigma and be part of a world phenomena.

National UFO Conference
Website: www.UFOcongress.com
The Guinness World Record holding largest UFO convention. Talk about great energy and friendly people.

Alien Cosmic Expo: Conference on Extraterrestrial Life
Website: aliencosmicexpo.com
An exciting line-up of speakers, UFO experts and researchers. Great opportunities for learning with such a world-class line-up.

Glastonbury Symposium
Website: WWW.glastonburysymposium.co.uk
One of Britain's long established and most acclaimed "alternative" annual 3-day conference of enlightening talks with a Sacred Sites Tour. I popped in for this convention one day, didn't stay but a minute, when I was visiting Glastonbury.

I usually spent most of my time sitting in the nearby crop circles and exploring the historic sites of Glastonbury, but it is definitely on my "bucket list," to return one day soon.

The Scotland UFO & Paranormal Conference
Website: https://www.facebook.com/scottishufoand
paranormalconference2016
Lectures on UFO's and the Paranormal.
Some of the best speakers in the UK.
Can't wait to attend this one.

Oh by the Way...

If you have any questions, thoughts, added information, resources and ideas on how I can improve this
book and your reading experience, or if you have a
question I can help you with, I invite you to leave a
comment on my website or email. If I don't have the
answer, I will try to find someone who can help you.

If you would like to be on my mailing list to be on
the pre-order book list and/or to be the first to hear
about upcoming classes, events or tour dates, simply go
to my websites:

www.BarbaraJeanLindsey.com
www.Facebook.com/DyingFortheLight
www.EsotericUniversity.com

I will respond personally, as soon as possible, as I
do appreciate your comments.

One More Thing ...

If you like what you have read, I would appreciate it if you would leave a testimonial at:

www.Amazon.com

Thank you in advance...
-Barbara Jean

Made in the USA
Las Vegas, NV
11 May 2023

71926175R00075